D0482827

Ketchup
Is a
Vegetable

O'Bryant, Robin.
Ketchup is a vegetable
: and other lies moms t
c2011.
33305229325570
bk   07/17/14

Ketchup Is a Vegetable

· ·

And Other Lies Moms Tell Themselves

Robin O'Bryant

St. Martin's Griffin

New York

To Uncle Lou:

For seeing a gift in me
it took thirty years to find on my own.

To Zeb, Aubrey, Emma, and Sadie:

You are the loves of my life. Without the four of you
I have no story worth telling.

KETCHUP IS A VEGETABLE. Copyright © 2011, 2014 by Robin O'Bryant. All rights reserved. Printed in the United States of America. For information, address St. Martin's Press, 175 Fifth Avenue, New York, N.Y. 10010.

www.stmartins.com

The Library of Congress Cataloging-in-Publication Data is available upon request.

ISBN 978-1-250-05414-2 (trade paperback)
ISBN 978-1-4668-5719-3 (e-book)

First published in the United States by Greenforge Books in 2011
Published by St. Martin's Griffin as an e-original in October 2013

St. Martin's Griffin books may be purchased for educational, business, or promotional use. For information on bulk purchases, please contact Macmillan Corporate and Premium Sales Department at 1-800-221-7945, extension 5442, or write special markets@macmillan.com.

First St. Martin's Griffin Paperback Edition: April 2014

10 9 8 7 6 5 4 3 2 1

Contents

Introduction

In an effort to keep you from totally losing your mind while reading this book and wondering, Who is this woman? Where does she live and she has HOW many daughters? I thought I'd start by telling you a little about myself.

I grew up in Jasper, Alabama, and married my husband, Zeb, when he was nineteen and I was twenty years old. (If my children are reading this, we were really twenty-seven. Ahem.) In 1998, with a teeny tiny U-Haul truck, we moved to Fort Worth, Texas, where we lived and worked for two years. Then we loaded up a slightly less teeny truck with our stuff in 2000 and moved to Auburn, Alabama, to finish our bachelor's degrees. We lived in Auburn for five years while I got a degree in nursing, worked as an ER nurse, and had our first child, Aubrey, (who was NOT named after the school) in 2004.

We moved to Savannah, Georgia, in November of 2005 for Zeb's job (we actually needed a big truck this time), where our second daughter, Emma, was born. (Are you confused yet? I knew I should've made a diagram.) We lived in Savannah for two years, then moved again in 2007 for Zeb's job. This time the move was to Mount Pleasant, South Carolina, a suburb of Charleston, for another two years. There, we had YET another girl baby—Sadie.

Still with me?

Zeb. Married. Texas. Auburn. Aubrey. Savannah. Emma. Charleston. Sadie.

Then my husband was offered a job that would allow him to work from corporate headquarters and not require that we move every two years. We hired professional movers with eighteen-wheelers and moved to Greenwood, Mississippi, in December of 2009. We made some friends, developed a social life, and quit making babies.

Most of these essays were written while living in Charleston and Greenwood while my children were tearing my house down around me. The essays in this book do not necessarily move chronologically, so if Aubrey is four in one essay and two in the next, just know it's because I thought this was the best order for the stories I had to tell.

And just to give you a little more insight into these crazy, wonderful people I get to call my family, I'm going to give you a little bio on each one.

Zeb: love of my life. Man of my dreams. He is seriously smart. He made his ACT cry. He can and will build anything from houses and hospitals to helicopter hangars and playhouses for little girls. He has taught our daughters to shoot BB guns while the girls were wearing princess dresses and high heels.

Aubrey: our firstborn. Blue-eyed, freckled, and with perfect strawberry-blond ringlets. When she was two to four, I wondered if she would break me, but she has the sweetest, most sensitive heart. She is the Boss of her sisters and occasionally of me. She can't stand for anyone to get their feelings hurt and scolds the entire family when we laugh at someone falling down on *America's Funniest Home Videos*. And once they are in high school, it will be Aubrey who tells the truth and reveals where Emma actually is . . . as opposed to where she tells me she is.

Emma: she's always been a tiny little thing, all arms and legs. Blue eyes and white-blond hair that curls up when she's climbing trees or disassembling her daddy's Harley. She has MacGyver's motor skills, and she's not afraid to use them. Chances are if something is broken in our house, she did it. She loves to know how things work and will often take stuff apart just to see if she can figure it out. Emma is calculating and crafty. I've got Aubrey praying with me about her teenage years.

Sadie: my baaaaay-by. Sadie is laughter, dimpled cheeks, and pure, unadulterated fun in a toddler-shaped package. White-blond hair that is always hanging into her wild blue eyes and a dedicated tormentor of her sisters—although in this book she mostly drools, eats, sleeps, and poops.

Welcome to the chaos I call life.

1
· · · · · · · ·

Birth Control? Yes, Please

I should have been on the beach with my kids, building sand castles and frolicking in the ocean. (Okay, yelling at them to stop eating sand and getting sunburned.) I should have been packing a picnic to enjoy in one of hundreds of parks in the Charleston area, a picnic my children would have totally ignored while they cried for another child's Happy Meal, but still. I should have been at our neighborhood pool, providing first aid the teenage lifeguards were incapable of rendering themselves while praying one of my children didn't poop in the pool. I should have been anywhere but where I was—sitting on the toilet doubled over with stomach cramps.

I was eleven weeks pregnant and, ahem, a little backed up.

I was stuck on the toilet as my four-year-old and two-year-old had free rein of the house. The amount of destruction Aubrey and Emma are capable of under adult supervision is astounding, but I was going to be here for a while, and they were running rampant through my house. I was so consumed with my stomach cramps that I didn't even have time to be properly terrified at what was probably going on in the next room.

My legs were just starting to go numb from loss of circulation from sitting on the toilet seat for so long when Aubrey, my oldest, came running into the bathroom.

"Momma, what are you doing?"

"I'm trying to go potty, Aubrey."

"Ohhhhh, it's taking a long time, huh, Momma?"

"Yes, it is."

"Do you need help, Momma?"

"No, honey . . ." I trailed off as another wave of stomach cramps and nausea swept over me. Aubrey saw my pain as an open door and yelled, "Mommy, can I have some candy?"

"If you can reach it in the pantry you can have whatever you want."

She ran out of the room as fast as her little feet would carry her, before I could change my mind, and I heard her yell to her sister, "Momma said we could have candy! Come on, Emma!"

What the hell had I been thinking when I decided to have another baby? It always seemed like a good idea until the nausea hit, which for me usually starts the day I pee on a stick and continues twenty-four hours a day until I hit the thirteen-week mark. My morning sickness had gotten progressively worse with each of my pregnancies. And now, I was pregnant, in charge of two toddlers, and even the slightest movement made me want to barf up my toenails. My husband was at work, all of my family was a good ten-hour drive away, and since we had recently moved again, I didn't have a single friend I could call. Not one I could discuss my bowel habits with, anyway.

I had never dealt with this particular pregnancy symptom before, and I was at a loss. I had tried everything I knew to do as a nurse . . . drinking fluids, eating prunes, taking stool soften-ers. I knew what the next step was, and I was horrified. My hus-band and I have been through a lot together, but we are definitely a "poop with the door closed" kind of couple.

This pregnancy had brought me to a new low. I yelled from my throne for one of the girls to bring me the phone and dialed my husband's number.

"Hey! 'Sup?" he asked cheerfully.

I started sobbing as I uttered words I never thought I would say to the man I love. "I need you to bring me an enema."

I couldn't believe I had actually said the words out loud. But there was no way I could load two kids into car seats and wrangle them through a pharmacy to purchase what I needed. I waited in the bathroom while Aubrey and Emma sat on the edge of the bathtub eating Pop-Tarts and staring at me doubled over on the toilet.

I heard Zeb's car pull in the driveway and almost cried again when he opened the bathroom door with a bag from our drug-store in his hand.

"Do you need some help?" he asked.

"Yes, take your kids and let me be sick by myself. And please, please don't ever get me pregnant again," I said. I snatched the bag out of his hand, pushed all three of my family members out of the bathroom, and locked the door behind them.

There are a lot of things I said I would never do when I had kids. I swore I would never say, "Because I said so," "Don't you make me pull this car over!" or "You just wait until your daddy gets home!" I would never "let myself go," have petrified French fries on the floor of my car, or wear pajama pants to the grocery store, and I would never, ever drive a minivan. The only one of those things I've stuck to is not driving the minivan, but it's not by choice. I fantasize about my own minivan on a daily basis, complete with automatic sliding doors, enough cargo space to haul a dead body (you never know, right?), and stale fries on the floor.

I used to think I wanted four kids. This was, of course, before I had one and realized how much work was involved. I was convinced at eighteen years old that I would have four perfect little stair-steps, all exactly two years apart; two boys and two girls. (And, yes, I was a little type A.)

I heard people talk about how hard it was to be a parent, but I babysat all the time. Being a babysitter and being a mom are practically the same thing, right?

I thought I knew. I had no idea. The thing you can't explain to someone who doesn't have children is how constant being a parent actually is. It is more than twenty-four hours a day, seven days a week . . . if that's even possible.

Children, toddlers especially, have boundless energy with which they can torture their parents. Hell, if all I had to do all day was color, watch *Blue's Clues,* eat a snack, and nap, I'd have boundless energy, too. But, no, I am the one getting out the crayons, trying to keep my children from consuming crayons, picking up broken crayons, and putting away the crayons. (And while I'm on the subject, why don't those folks at Crayola either add some vitamins and minerals to their product or make them taste bad? My kids love eating them, and I'm tired of telling them no and having to buy more. Put up or shut up, Crayola. Fortify them or make them taste bad. This isn't rocket science.)

Unless you want your children to be completely stinking rotten, not only do you have to tell them no on a regular basis, you have to mean it and to be ready and willing to back it up. All the energy they conserve while napping, snacking, and playing is ammunition to defeat us, their parents, who have been busy behind the scenes keeping the house from falling apart. Even though you are exhausted, you have to win. Once you have thrown down the gauntlet and made a rule, if your child breaks it 200 times in one day, you have to correct them 201 times.

Now, I'll be the first one to admit to occasionally ignoring bad behavior. If my two oldest are in another room, making a mess without cleaning up one they have already made, and I am actually getting something done, such as cooking dinner or doing laundry, I may have occasionally pretended I couldn't hear them so I could finish the task at hand and dealt with their bad behavior after I was finished. You say, "Lazy parenting." I say, "Priorities, priorities, priorities."

I do deal with the behavior. I just act shocked when I walk into their room, like I didn't realize what was going on. I also recognize that I can't keep this up forever because they will eventually figure it out. But for now, a mom's gotta do what a mom's gotta do.

And have you ever attempted reasoning with a toddler? Even explaining to them why their behavior is wrong can be exhausting.

"But why, Momma? But why?"

I have tried and tried and tried to be patient, to be an attentive parent, to answer each "why" with love and long suffering . . . to avoid the phrase I detested so much as a child: "Because I said so."

"GIRLS! Quit jumping on the bed!"

"Why, Mommy, why?"

"Because it's dangerous."

"Why, Mommy, why?"

"Because you could fall and break your arm or your neck

or impale yourself on the posts sticking up out of the footboard . . ."

"Why, Mommy, why?"

"Because you are jumping on the bed . . ."

"Why, Mommy, why?"

"Because you are being bad. Stop. Jumping. On. The. Bed."

"Why, Mommy, why?"

"BECAUSE I SAID SO."

It's unfortunate, but it really is the only phrase that can stop one of these maddening conversations in its tracks.

Another thing I knew nothing about was the selective hearing children seem to experience as they enter their preschool years. Anything you say to another adult (especially regarding another adult) can be repeated verbatim by your children. Anything you say directly to your child must automatically be repeated—at least twice.

"Emma, stop unrolling the toilet paper all over the bathroom," I'll say clearly, standing less than fourteen inches away from her.

"HUH? What you said, Momma?" she'll ask with one hand cupped around her ear and leaning in . . . as if she actually cannot hear me.

Their selective hearing will often lead to my wondering if I actually spoke out loud or if I was just really concentrating on what I was going to say.

"Test one, two . . . testing . . . is this thing on?" I'll say as I pretend to check a microphone, which usually leads to zero response from anyone in my house and occasionally makes me think that they really can hear, but I apparently don't know how to make words come out of my mouth.

I just didn't realize B.C. (Before Children) how much work it takes to maintain some sort of order in your house. You are constantly cleaning, battling for good manners and good behavior and refereeing fights between siblings, trying to teach values and spend quality time with each child and your spouse. It is exhausting. (Quick soapbox moment here for you "animal people"—having a pet, even a dog, is not the same as having children. Case in point: you can lock your "baby" in a cage or take it outside, lock the door, and ignore it for a few hours. Parents cannot, unless we would like a cage of our very own.)

Even with all of this, when I was pregnant with my third child I still wasn't sure I was "done." After I had my second child, I didn't feel like our family was complete; it felt like someone was missing. And, to be honest, I was worried I would be sad when my baby-making days were over. My husband was satisfied with his three daughters, but throughout my third pregnancy I speculated about what would happen if I wanted another child and my husband did not. I had looked forward to being pregnant and having babies my whole life and wondered if I would be depressed to say good-bye to those days and begin a new chapter with my family.

All my concerns about wanting more children quickly vaporized when I was introduced to life as a mother to three. As soon as I held Sadie Plum in my arms, I knew my whole family was present and accounted for. I breathed a huge sigh of relief as all the pressure and expectations I had placed on myself for so long faded away.

I began the cleansing process of giving away maternity clothes and baby items as Sadie outgrew them. The idea of getting into shape and finally being able to replace my very dated wardrobe was intoxicating. As soon as a pair of pants or a shirt was deemed too large for me, it immediately went into my giveaway pile.

Things at my house were crazy but fulfilling. I loved being a mother to my three daughters, but I was still quite positive my baby-making days were behind me and smiled at myself in the mirror as I took my birth control pill every night.

Until one evening I stumbled into the bathroom to take my pill and couldn't find them. It was a Friday evening, and I was exhausted from a week of entertaining my children in the summer heat. I dug around in my drawer and in my jewelry box, just in case a "little helper" had stashed them somewhere, before I finally gave up and decided to go to bed and look for them in the morning.

Of course, the next morning I was woken up as Aubrey, my four-year-old, and Emma, my two-year-old, wrestled for the spot next to me in my bed and, in the process, almost threw me onto the floor. It was two days later when I finally remembered I still hadn't found my birth control pills and began frantically searching my bathroom.

I called a family meeting.

"Everyone in Mommy and Daddy's bathroom RIGHT NOW!"

Aubrey and Emma walked calmly into the bathroom, followed by their sweet daddy.

"What's up?" he asked.

"Aubrey and Emma were in our bathroom the other day playing with my makeup, and I haven't been able to find my birth control since then . . ."

I didn't have to say one more word. My husband transformed from a laid-back, fly-by-the-seat-of-your-pants kind of guy to a drill sergeant.

"You will find Mommy's medicine and you will not STOP until you find it! Do you understand?"

Aubrey spoke up. "Oh! It's okay, Mommy, you can do it! Just be very patient and keep on looking."

My husband said, "I don't think you understand. No one is leaving this room until we find Mommy's medicine."

"Oh," she replied.

As soon as Emma realized this was not a test but serious business, she opened the cabinet and plucked my medicine from its hiding spot.

"Here you go, Mommy!" she said proudly.

I couldn't have been happier to see those pills if I was stranded in the Sahara and someone offered me a Cherry Limeade from Sonic—one of those route 44 ones, the ones that are big enough to swim in. It might be time to start researching other birth control options. They couldn't find and hide an IUD from me . . . could they?

2
· · · · · · ·

It Ain't as Easy as It Looks

We've seen it in the movies and on TV a million times. The perfectly pregnant woman (who just has a baby bump and is skin and bones everywhere else) wakes up in the middle of the night and tells her husband, "It's time." He rushes around like a nincompoop. He can't find his shoes, his keys, or his suitcase, while she does deep breathing. They hurry to the hospital, where it is too late for an epidural. Thank God they took Lamaze classes! She can now push a person out of her body by doing a few "hoo-hoo-hees."

Then, miraculously, the baby appears, pink and clean and looking about three months old. The now perfectly serene mommy, who will have no trouble whatsoever fitting into her size 4 jeans, puts the baby to her breast with a smile and a contented sigh, while the new daddy beams dotingly over her shoulder.

Ladies, Hollywood is doing us no favors.

First off, I would like to say that anyone who is skinny and pregnant does not deserve an epidural; in fact, any such woman deserves hemorrhoids. Secondly, there is a way to ensure that it is never too late for an epidural. My advice is starting at thirty-seven weeks you should go to your obstetrician's office daily and claim to be in labor and tell them you are ready for your epidural. They are not going to send you home without checking you because they are afraid of a little thing called a malpractice lawsuit. Eventually, you will actually be in labor and be able to get said epidural. I do not understand, nor do I want to understand, the level of masochism involved with someone wanting to give birth Laura Ingalls Wilder style. I've had three babies and it hurt. All that "hee-hee-hooing" ain't all it's cracked up to be.

And another thing, your baby is not going to be pink or clean. Not at first anyway. Your child is going to look like she went to Paula Deen's house, was confused with the Thanksgiving turkey, and got basted with butter. And if that kid comes out the way God intended her to, she's probably going to look like she was in a barroom brawl, as well. I cried when I saw Aubrey for the first time, partly because I was a mother and here was my firstborn child and partly because her nose was crooked.

Nobody told me when I was pregnant that some babies don't know how to breastfeed, and I was finishing nursing school and had worked in Labor and Delivery for two years while I was in school. I felt like I had been totally duped.

Breastfeeding was the most frustrating experience of my life. I had a screaming, hungry baby and a bowling ball–sized boob full of milk. It seemed simple. But it wasn't. Aubrey didn't know how to latch on properly, and when we finally figured that out, she would fall asleep every time I tried to feed her. I went to the "lactation consultant" in tears and showed her my nipples; they looked like something out of a science fiction movie.

"Have you been putting the lanolin on them like I showed you?" she asked snidely.

I don't recall ever wanting to hit someone so badly in my entire life. That would be like telling the victim of a gunshot wound to put a Band-Aid on a gaping wound. Yes, Einstein, I had been using the damn lanolin. I was pretty sure my right nipple was going to fall off, and wondered if medical science had yet to invent a prosthetic nipple, or if I would have to plod through the rest of my life looking like I had attempted to nurse a grizzly bear.

Thanks to her fabulous guidance and direction, I ended up with mastitis, which is a full-blown infection with fever and chills. Exactly what you need when you have a newborn baby and are sleeping in one-and-a-half-hour increments.

I endured. I thought that's what mothers were supposed to do. I cried every time I had to feed Aubrey and dreaded the next feeding in between. I said four-letter words that I didn't even know I knew. I was afraid she was going to develop an eating disorder because I cried every time I fed her. I had horrible daydreams of her crying through every meal for the rest of her life. I could see her sitting at the table, meal after meal, year after year, crying while she ate. "Aubrey, honey, what is wrong?" "I don't know," she would hiccup, "something about eating just makes me so . . . so sad!"

I talked about nursing with all of my family and friends who had breastfed their own babies. I kept waiting and wanting so badly for somebody to tell me it was okay to quit, but they were all so damn supportive that I felt guilty for wanting to quit.

I went to Dr. Alverson, my ob-gyn, for my six-week checkup. I knew him from working in the hospital as a nurse. He walked in the door with his assistant, slapped me on the back, and said, "So, how's the breastfeeding going?" I lost all composure. Six weeks' worth of frustration, anger, and lack of sleep came gushing out all over my poor doctor.

"OH GOD!" I cried. "It's awful! I hate it! Both of my nipples are a bloody mess. I cry every time I have to feed her and dread the next feeding for the two hours in between!"

"Why didn't you call me? You don't think I know anything about boobs?" he asked.

"I went to the lactation consultant at the hospital, and she told me to use lanolin. I even went to a . . . a . . . a . . . breastfeeding support meeting." Which, by the by, had been a horrible decision on my part. I was uncomfortable enough sitting in the privacy of my own home, whipping out the Big Berthas every two to three hours, and trying to force Aubrey to open her mouth, stay awake, and suck, but breastfeeding in a group with other women just seemed perverse.

I should have realized the meeting wasn't for me when I first read the sign:

Breastfeeding Support Group:
Meets every Tuesday at noon in the dayroom.
Bring a sack lunch, drinks provided.

Drinks provided? In a meeting about breastfeeding? Got milk? I should have realized then and there that this was going to be a bunch of granola-eating, patchouli-wearing, übermommies. But I am a glutton for punishment, so I went to the meeting, where I was peer pressured by the lactation consultant to breastfeed my child in front of a large group of strangers. I'm sure you've probably seen women discreetly breastfeeding before, but when one of your breasts weighs more than your baby . . . it's kind of difficult to keep things on the down low. I almost had to ask the woman sitting next to me to get up and move so I would have room to prop part of my breast up on her armrest.

"I tried, Dr. Alverson! I tried to do everything I possibly could! I wanted to breastfeed. I thought my body would know how to do this! I thought my baby would know how to do this! I thought the lactation consultant knew what she was talking about, but she made me breastfeed in front of strangers, and I'm about to lose a nipple!" I hiccuped as his nurse handed me a tissue, and I blew my nose.

My fabulous doctor listened to my monologue of breastfeeding woes and introduced me to a plethora of breastfeeding gadgets that had my boobs healed up in no time, except for the permanent scar I have on my right nipple. (Just thought I'd throw that out there, in case I ever go missing and someone needs to identify my body. I watch *Law & Order;* I know how these things work.)

My sweet mother-in-law, who nursed five babies herself, bought me a book in the midst of my troubles from the La Leche League, or the Nursing Nazis, as I lovingly refer to them. I was so grateful for the book because I was obviously doing everything wrong and had no idea how to fix it. But I'm also pretty sure that I got the wrong book. I wasn't nearly as dedicated as these people were. There was a chapter on tandem nursing. For those of you who don't know what that is, that would be nursing your toddler and your newborn at the same time. (Yes, there were pictures, and yes, I witnessed this in person at the meeting of my breastfeeding support group.)

If you have the gross motor skills to unhook your mother's nursing bra, you need to be drinking out of a cup and off the tit. These people think the breast is the answer to everything. Basically, if your baby cries, that is what he wants. "Offer the breast, offer the breast, offer the breast." I had no intention of ever being a pacifier. I'd use the Big Berthas to feed this kid, but that was it. (You know you have the Big Berthas when you have to special order your bras on the Internet and your husband can wear one cup on his head like a yarmulke.)

The end of the road came shortly after that, when I woke up one morning and my three-month-old had thrush. "Hell to the no," I told myself. "I will not be getting another infection." I speed-dialed my doctor.

"Wade Alverson," he answered.

"Dr. Alverson, it's Robin O'Bryant . . . I woke up this morning and Aubrey has thrush in her mouth. I've HAD it. I refuse to get thrush. That is just disgusting. So, I quit. I'm done. What can I do to wrap this up?"

"Bind your breasts with an ACE bandage, use ice packs and cabbage leaves," he said.

"Excuse me, cabbage leaves?" I asked skeptically. "What exactly am I supposed to do with cabbage leaves?"

"Put them in your bra and bind your breasts," he said.

"Wade." I used his first name so he would know I was really serious. "Don't mess with me. Are you for real?"

"Absolutely. It works."

Here's the dealio: there is some sort of enzyme in the actual cabbage leaf that helps when you are engorged with milk. It works when your milk first comes in (but you are supposed to use them sparingly if you plan to breastfeed, so it doesn't affect your milk supply), and it works especially well when you have had enough and decide it's time to wean, whenever that may be. Not only is the enzyme helpful, but if you keep your cabbage in the refrigerator, the leaves are cold and just happen to be shaped the right way to fit in your brassiere.

Helpful hint: if you are especially blessed in this area, you might tell your husband to get the biggest head of cabbage he can find so that you don't have to put small little pieces everywhere but can just use one large leaf per boob. If not, you will end up with what is essentially coleslaw in your bra and then you will have to pick small dried-up pieces of cabbage from all over your house because they fall out of the bottom of your bra. Not that I know. I'm just saying . . . it seems perfectly logical that that could happen to someone. If, say, their husband bought a head of cabbage the size of a brussels sprout.

So cabbage leaves it was, and although I spent the next seven to ten days smelling like Chinese stir-fry, I enjoyed my time with Aubrey immeasurably more after that. I still wish I had given myself permission to quit sooner. I wasted so much time hating it. I had much better experiences with my next two children. But I learned a valuable lesson: the breast isn't best for everyone.

And although I have continued to breastfeed all three of my children for some length of time, I hate it with every fiber of my being and here are the top ten reasons why:

1. It hurts.
2. My boobs get so big that they totally eclipse my child's head when I'm feeding her.
3. My boobs are so big that Victoria can no longer keep my secrets.
4. No one else can help you or do it for you.

5. People give you dirty looks when you do it in public, even if you shove your kid up your shirt and cover up with a blanket.

6. Breast pumps make you feel like an actual cow. Mooooo.

7. My boobs are so big that I lost a pacifier once and found it that night when I took off my bra.

8. You can get tennis elbow from it, which does provide you with prescription painkillers, which you can't take because you're breastfeeding.

9. You can't drink unless you want to have to buy the "breast screen" test strips at Target to screen your milk for alcohol. Purchasing said strips is only going to lead to more dirty looks. The first time I saw them I wanted to buy a box of strips, a bottle of wine, go home, and pump, just to see what would happen.

10. Boob sweat is disgusting (think blue cheese gone bad or "rurnt," as we like to say in Alabama). You have to bathe or your kid is going to smell like it every time you feed her. If you are a B cup or under, you can't relate and I don't care or feel sorry for you.

The good things about breastfeeding:

1. It's supposedly good for your kid (even though Aubrey was only breastfed for three months and is never sick and Emma was breastfed for eleven months and is always sick).

2. It's free. (This is mostly why I do it . . . don't judge me.)

3

. . . .

Awkward Naked Moments

I've never thought of myself as particularly modest. I never had a humiliating experience changing clothes in the locker room for gym class. I grew up having my own bedroom and bathroom and didn't have to duke it out with my siblings over a lack of privacy—unlike my husband, who shared a bathroom with his four siblings and his parents. It's still not uncommon for someone to walk in the door and take a quick potty break when you are in the shower at his parents' house. It's how he was raised, and even though I was raised differently, I felt I adjusted quite well to life as an O'Bryant. I didn't mind if someone came in the bathroom to pee while I was in the shower, providing they didn't peek behind the shower curtain, flush the toilet, or actually take care of more serious bathroom business.

I worked my way through college as a tech in Labor and Delivery. I assisted with C-sections and postpartum tubals, set up trays of instruments for vaginal deliveries, and saw a lot of babies being born. It was a beautiful thing, and every delivery made me look forward to having my own children and consider what type of experience I would want for the birth of my first child.

Would I want a natural delivery with scented candles and my husband massaging my back? Mmmm, tempting—but no. An epidural and gin rummy sounded like a much better birth plan for me.

Would I want my mother, my sister, my father, my husband, my mother-in-law, and my high school youth-group leader all holding my hand and chanting together, "PUSH, Robin, PUSH"? Again, tempting, but no. My husband and I made this baby all by ourselves, and that was the way we wanted to bring her into the world.

Because I worked in Labor and Delivery for a couple of years, I knew and worked with all the ob-gyns in town. All of them. I chose my doctor very carefully, and made it clear to the receptionist at his office that I would not be making the rounds at their office showing my lady bits to anyone and everyone there. I would see my doctor and my doctor only for appointments, but would be fine delivering with whoever was on call when I went into labor. I had to look these people in the eye on a daily basis—in the operating room, no less—and I just didn't think they all needed to see my Britney.

Our extended family lived about three hours away from Zeb and me, and my plan was to call them from the hospital after I got settled in but right before I had the baby. Because, you know, things like delivering your first child are so predictable. The plan was that I would get my epidural, kick my husband's butt at gin rummy (like I always do), have a baby and possibly a snack, and be ready to greet my family when they arrived. I was not going to be one of those people who had ten people standing around their bed staring at them while they just lay there and prayed for cervical dilation.

Nope, not this girl. No, this girl ended up with eleven people standing around staring at her. Turns out labor can take a really long time—like long enough for eleven of your closest family members to drive three hours.

My brother commented while staring at the fat girl in the bed, "You seem so calm and peaceful."

"Yeah, you would be, too, if you couldn't feel anything from the waist down. I haven't been this comfortable in nine months."

As my labor progressed, my nurse friends kindly escorted everyone to the waiting room so I could continue to kill my husband at rummy—I mean, push and stuff.

Eventually, I had to put my cards down to have a baby, and when I did I realized I really wanted my momma in the room with us. I was surprised because I had always thought it would just be my husband and me, but at that moment I wanted her to be there.

Zeb and my mother stood on either side of the bed, chatting as my epidural wore off and I began to realize what all the screaming is about on TLC's *A Baby Story*. I actually had to interrupt the conversation they were carrying on over my head to remind them to focus and said, "Do you mind maybe CHEERING or something while I push an actual human out of my vagina?!"

Aubrey was born healthy and without any complications, but she brought with her a problem I had never seen coming. I didn't even know they existed. But after the birth of my child, I began experiencing Awkward Naked Moments.

Being naked while I was in labor wasn't a big deal. I mean, I was having a baby and was sort of preoccupied with the wonderfulness of my epidural slipping away just when I needed it most. And technically I wasn't completely naked; I was wearing a hospital gown. I didn't have time to daydream about all the awkwardness that was to follow.

Obviously, I had been naked in front of both my mother and my husband before—but, somehow, being naked in front of both of them at the same time had set some sort of precedent. A line had been crossed, and there was no going back.

Once Aubrey was old enough to take a real bath, I would often put her in the bathtub with me and call to my husband or my mother (if she happened to be in town visiting) to come and get her so I could finish bathing. This somehow became a cattle call, signaling everyone in my house to come into the bathroom to watch Aubrey splash and coo—which, again, would have been perfectly fine, if I hadn't been naked.

"Hey, I'm going to go get in the bathtub and bathe Aubrey. Will one of you come and get her when I'm finished?" I would ask my mother and husband.

They nodded in agreement as I marched my happy postpartum self to the bathroom for a few minutes of bath-time play with my baby. Aubrey loved to be free in the water. She would become animated and giggly as she splashed and kicked her fat little legs. The louder her coos and baby talk became, the harder I would laugh and inevitably . . . they would come.

Zeb and Shuggie, my mother, couldn't resist the siren song of Aubrey's squeals and laughter, and they would come running to make sure they weren't missing out on a milestone of any kind.

I was fine as long as they weren't both in the room. To have my husband or my mother in the bathroom watching Aubrey splash around was fine, but both of them? It just felt deviant.

"What's she doing?" my mother yelled as she skidded into

the bathroom. "I can hear her laughing over the TV in the den!"

"She's just kicking her arms and legs, every time she splashes water in her face she laughs hysterically . . ." I trailed off as Aubrey splashed herself in the face again and made me and my mother cackle with her.

"What am I missing?" Zeb asked as he swung around the corner into the bathroom, drawn, no doubt, by the sounds of our laughter.

"OH! Zeb, it is the SWEETEST THING I'VE EVER SEEN! Every time she splashes water in her face, she just laughs and laughs! Show him, Robin," my mother answered him.

They turned to me in slow motion as I moved my baby to try to strategically use her to cover all of my naughty bits, but covering a postpartum body with a three-month-old is sort of impossible. At the time, one of the Big Berthas alone easily outweighed my child by a good pound or two.

I tried to stay calm. I mean, what's the problem? I had asked for one of them to come and get her, and, so what, they both came . . . no big deal, right?

"Hey, baby! Hey, little girl!" Zeb leaned over the tub to coo at Aubrey. She grinned her toothless grin and splashed, getting water in her face and leading to more hysterical laughter.

"Aubrey, Aubrey!" my mother sang. "Look at you, you sweet, fat little thing!"

By this point, Shuggie and Zeb were leaning over the tub and in Aubrey's face as I continued to desperately try to use my child to shield my coo-coo from scrutiny.

"Zeb! Zeb, go get the camera. This is just too sweet! You've got to take pictures. Look at all those fat rolls!"

Fat rolls? Pictures? I was pretty sure my mother was talking about Aubrey's fat rolls, but I was horrified and too stunned to even speak. Here I was trying to get one or both of them out of the room with my kid so I could shave my legs, and possibly my privacy now that everyone was going to be looking at it on a daily basis, and they wanted pictures?

"Um, I think Aubrey is ready to get out . . . she seems sorta, uhh, tired or hungry or something . . . ," I said as Aubrey continued to babble and coo with happiness.

"Oh, she's fine," my mother said dismissively as Zeb returned with the camera.

They leaned farther over the tub and my mother began jumping around and trying desperately to make Aubrey laugh again so her smile could be captured on camera. It was time for me to change my strategy. I could no longer use her to shield my body, because the closer I held her, the more likely I was to appear in the pictures with her. Naked.

I held Aubrey underneath her head and her tiny little bottom as far away from me as possible, completely exposing my Britney, and tried to keep the Big Berthas from floating into the frame.

While my boobs floated around on top of the water somewhere close to my knees, I was trying to think of a nice way to tell them to get the hell out. Really, they didn't both need to go, but one of them did. I wasn't picky—either one of them leaving would have eliminated all weirdness. But I couldn't afford to piss anyone off. Because, let's face it, I had a brand-new baby, and I wanted as much sleep as I could possibly get and wasn't sure if they left how far they would actually go or when they would come back. I needed them, but I had to put an end to Awkward Naked Moments.

It progressed to the point that I would be in the shower or in my bedroom changing clothes, no cute, fat, naked baby involved to justify their behavior, and my husband and my mother would inevitably wander in just to chat. Not about anything in particular, just shooting the breeze—what's for dinner, that type of thing.

Breastfeeding didn't help matters (reason #432 that I hate it). Whipping my boobs out every two and a half to three hours was only further evidence to them that I was free and comfortable with my nakedness and inevitably led to many more Awkward Naked Moments.

I almost said something several times, but the conversations I was rehearsing in my head just sounded so juvenile:

"I know you have both seen me naked before, but that was at different times. I don't mind being seen naked by either of you, but I am not emotionally stable enough to handle both of you seeing me naked at the same time. It's just weird. Unless I'm in labor, which means there will be drugs involved and I won't really care."

In my mind, I pictured them looking at each other like I had lost my mind and asking me what I meant that it was "weird." I could just hear my mother: "ROBIN, you are being ridiculous! You should be glad that anybody comes when you call for help, much less two of us! It's not like we haven't seen you naked before, for crying out loud. Quit acting like a spoiled brat!"

But come on, people, being seen au naturel by your husband, i.e., your luvah, and being seen by your mother, the person who changed your diapers and brought you into this world, are two totally different states of nakedness that should never, ever take place simultaneously. (Take my word on this.)

I was in my bedroom in a state of undress one afternoon

talking through the wall to my husband and my mother, who were in the living room. I had the door slightly ajar so they could hear me, when all of a sudden the door opened and they were both standing in the hallway. Zeb was eating a sandwich, and my mother was just chattering away.

It was the sandwich that did it. It was one thing for them to stalk my nakedness when the baby was involved, but that sandwich really pushed me over the edge. It's hard enough to feel sexy in front of your husband when you weigh more than he does, your breasts are bigger than his head, and he has seen you push a baby out of your Britney. But the fact that Zeb could stand there casually observing my nakedness with my mother whilst eating a ham sandwich and wiping mustard off of his chin simply blinded me with rage.

I snapped.

"I can be naked in front of one of you at a time! Do you hear me? ONE! Not both of you! It freaks me out, and it has to stop now! No more family bath time! No more nudie photo shoots! No more coming in here when I'm changing! No more eating while I'm naked! No more! ONE AT A TIME!"

I slammed the door in their faces as they stood there with their jaws hanging open, and then I finished changing. I was so relieved my Britney wasn't going to be making any more cameos in Aubrey's baby book that I didn't even care if they thought I was crazy.

4

· · · · · · ·

Baby Blues

As women, most of us look forward to the day when we will have our own children. We can't wait to take them home, bathe them, feed them, and dress them up. We should have known that if PMS is what precedes our monthly cycle, then all hell is liable to break loose after we go through the birth process.

I was elated when I found out I was pregnant with my first child. I couldn't wait to be a mother. I did the same things most expectant mommies do: I planned, I nested, I bought baby-name books. I couldn't wait to hold her in my arms and breathe in the scent of her, to see her tiny little fingers wrapped around mine. As clueless as I was, I even looked forward to breastfeeding— bonding with my baby as I gave her the best of everything I had to offer.

The days in the hospital after having her were like a Caribbean vacation . . . that exact memory may have been caused by the Percocet, but I really was in heaven. I treasured every touch, every smile, and every moment. I tried to let the nurses take her to the nursery so I could sleep, but the idea of her being away from me when she had been growing inside me for so long was almost painful.

One nurse convinced me to let her go for a few hours. "Come on, Robin, she'll be fine. I'll take her to the nursery so you won't wake up every time she breathes, and as soon as she's hungry I'll bring her right back to you."

"I don't know . . . I kind of like having her in here."

"Honey, you are going to have plenty of time with her when you go home. Let me help you while I can and take her to the nursery. You'll get a few hours of sleep and feel like a new woman."

"Okay, I guess. You'll bring her back if she gets hungry?"

"I sure will," she answered as she gently rolled the bassinet to the door, when Aubrey suddenly let out a cry, and I immediately recanted.

"WAIT! Just leave her with me." I realized, with startling clarity, that I was now her momma. I remembered in that one precise moment all of the times in my life when nothing would do but to be wrapped up in my mother's arms. In the smell of soap on sale and the loving assurance that no matter my troubles—I was not in them alone.

Aubrey's cry sent a shockwave through my nervous system that awakened the mother instinct in me. She was crying for her mother . . . she was crying for me. The nurse rolled her bassinet back into the room, placed my baby in my arms, and left. I held Aubrey as tears rolled down my cheeks and onto her tiny, flawless face.

We came home from the hospital to find my younger sister sitting at our kitchen table, surrounded by income tax forms for her first "real" job, and crying, "Do I pick zero or one? Why is this so hard? Why can't they just tell me what they want from me?!" I put my baby down, sat with my sister, and provided moral support as she filled out forms and chose her benefits package. I was an anchor in the midst of her storm. I was rolling with the punches. I was still myself. I was fine.

Five days later, our neighbor brought over a Sunday dinner fit for Paula Deen's table: pork chops, vegetables, three different salads, and dessert. I couldn't eat one bite. Aubrey was crying, like newborns do, and it was ripping my heart into shreds. I sat at our kitchen table, where I had been an anchor for my sister, and began to drown in a sea of hormones and unexplainable grief.

My husband carried our baby outside to sit on the porch swing and rocked her so I could eat. But I continued to sob. I couldn't stop. Hot tears slid down my cheeks. Zeb called my mother and told her we needed reinforcements and to come quick. He didn't know what to do with me. Hell, I didn't even know what to do with me.

I was overwhelmed by feelings of sadness, loneliness, grief, and guilt. The darkness was so tangible and real. It seems difficult now to even describe how hopeless I felt. Looking at Aubrey only increased my feelings of helplessness. What was I thinking when I decided to bring a life into this world? Her entire life was now my responsibility, and I felt the entire weight of it crushing down on my chest so heavily I wasn't sure I could take another breath.

I would sit and look at her for hours and cry, thinking about how dependent she was on me—without me she couldn't survive. If I didn't feed her, she would die. My slightest misstep or mistake could ruin her life. Her entire existence was in my hands, and it was all I could think about.

I cried as my phone rang and rang. I had caller ID and only

answered the phone if it was my mother or my sister. Interaction from the world outside my cocoon was too much to deal with; even listening to my friends and coworkers leave messages on my answering machine was overwhelming.

Beep. "Hi, Robin, it's Melissa." My manager from work. "Just calling to see how things are going and to let you know I'm here if you need anything." That was one of the most asinine statements I heard postpartum. If I needed anything? I needed everything. I needed someone to tell me to shower, someone to cook for me, do my laundry, hold my hand while I breastfed my child, go to the store for me. I didn't need vague offers of help. I needed someone to show up and do something. I needed someone to shake me until I snapped out of this funk.

Beep. "Hey, Robin, it's Lizzie . . . I, um, was just going to see if you were home. I made dinner for you guys and wanted to bring it by to you. I guess I'll just bring it over and see if your door is open? Okay, talk to you later." At least Lizzie was doing something, and although I was grateful for a meal I didn't have to prepare myself, part of me wanted to lock the door and hide from her. If I had a conversation with someone else, they would know. They would see how pathetic I was. They would see that I was a bad mother, upset, crying, and not fit to take care of my own child.

I watched the rise and fall of Aubrey's chest for hours after she and my husband went to sleep at night and prayed that another breath would come. I obsessed about too many covers in her bed, and the first night she spent in her own room I didn't sleep at all. I spent the entire night walking back and forth between our bedrooms making sure she was still alive.

I didn't want to hurt her or myself, but I couldn't get out of my mind all of the horrible things that could happen to her. Being a nurse didn't help at all. In fact, it probably only made things worse because I knew the statistics. Working in the hospital, I had seen things that most people never see. I had seen children who had been abused, disfigured in accidents, and victimized by pure circumstance. I was consumed with the thought that something similar could happen to my child.

I felt horrible about feeling horrible. How dare I be so sad when I had the most perfect life in the whole world? I had a wonderfully loving and supportive husband, a healthy child, and a job I loved waiting for me after my maternity leave. I had everything I had ever dreamed of in my entire life, and I was emotionally devastated. I was ashamed of myself for being so self-involved and sad.

Why? Why was I so sad? I loved my baby. I loved her more than words could express. I loved her so much that it made me physically ache. I cried for weeks. I avoided phone calls and visits from friends. What did I have to say to anybody? "Hey, I got what I always wanted, and now I can't quit sobbing long enough to brush my teeth or eat dinner. Thanks for dropping by."

I was a registered nurse. I knew this was postpartum depression; I knew it needed to be dealt with; I knew my doctor wouldn't dream of telling anyone about my private medical issues. But I was still so ashamed to admit it. I couldn't even bring myself to discuss it with my own mother. Talking about it with anyone seemed too overwhelming and difficult to even contemplate. (This was way before Tom Cruise made a complete jackass of himself for yelling at Matt Lauer about Brooke Shields's postpartum depression. So even though I'd like to, I can't blame the stigma I felt on that jerk.)

I was ashamed because I thought the depression somehow made me a failure as a mother. A good mother would be happy when her child was born. A good mother would leap right back into life. A good mother would want to leave the house so other people could see her child and coo over the newborn babe. I loved my baby, but I was perfectly content to stay in my house, in my bed or on my sofa with her for the next year, or years, just watching her breathe and making sure she was safe.

I waited an entire six weeks before I worked up the courage to tell my doctor. I wish someone had slapped me silly and said, "GIRL, get you some drugs for a few months and you'll be fine." But no one did, because no one knew. My doctor prescribed low-dose antidepressants, which I took for almost a year and then tapered off of under his direction. It felt so good to finally feel like myself again. I swore I would never allow myself to be sucked in and seduced by depression again.

Once I felt better, I could see how ridiculous my shame and guilt were, and I promised myself I would never fall that far again. I was fine after my second child, Emma, was born. Other than the typical sleep deprivation, there were no overwhelming emotions other than happiness.

After Sadie was born, I was fine for a few weeks until I felt that familiar sadness creeping over me again. I was cleaning the kitchen after dinner one evening with tears streaming down my face.

My husband walked up behind me at the kitchen sink, hugged me tightly against him, and said, "Baby, what's wrong?"

"NOTHING! I'm fine! I'm happy. I'm okay." My shoulders shook, and I could barely catch my breath because I was weeping so hard.

I called my doctor the very next day to begin taking medication.

My sister had her first baby only a month after I had my

third. Being the fab-a-lous big sister that I am, I sent her an e-mail and explained my past struggles with postpartum depression. I wrote, "I just don't want you to think there is something wrong with you if you are feeling this way. It is completely normal, and most people respond to treatment quickly and don't have to be on medication for very long. If you do feel this way, you're not alone; you can always talk to me. If you don't feel this way . . . well . . . I guess that means that I really am all alone . . .

"I'm KIDDING!" (See, I can be funny even when I'm depressed—it's a gift.)

You would think after all the monthly drama we go through, the carrying of the babies, the giving birth of the babies, the breastfeeding of the babies, that eventually God would feel sorry for us and give us a break! But, no, hormones are part of what makes us women and able to do the wonderful things our bodies do. While they are quite helpful in the person-making department, they can make us crazy in every other area of our lives. I would have given anything when I was dealing with postpartum depression to have known that I was normal. I wasn't losing my mind, and I was going to make it. Even though I felt alone when I was walking through it, I most certainly wasn't, and neither are you.

5

· · · · · · ·

Boob Sweat

I have a fascination with and fixation on boobs, not just my own. I am enthralled by your boobs just as much as I am by my very own. I wasn't aware of my obsession until a recent trip to Disney World. I found myself recognizing the people I passed in lines, as we wrapped back and forth between chains and handrails, not by their faces or their clothes, but by their boobs. I found myself passing the time by trying to guess what size bra the women were actually wearing and what size they should be wearing. I mentally fitted a few men for bras of their very own. I fantasized about recording clips of these people and sending them to the TV show *What Not to Wear,* which I would never really do because I keep asking all my friends to follow me around with a camera and send my pictures in, and I don't need any competition.

I realized during all my scientific research that Oprah's Bra Intervention a few years back had been a complete and udder failure. She said that something like 100 percent of women wear the wrong size bra and that she was on a mission to make every granny and housewife in the country get measured to buy a bra that lifts and separates.

There were braless boobs of every race and gender, for that matter. There were boobs representing every nationality—it was like a United Nations meeting for the boobs of the world. I kept waiting for Angelina Jolie to make an appearance to "show support."

I also realized while we were in Disney World that I was unwittingly passing on my obsession to my four-year-old. After a long day of swimming and playing at the hotel pool, half of the family was fast asleep. I was cuddled up in my mother's bed with her and Aubrey talking about what we were going to do the next day. I was wearing my nightgown, and Aubrey glanced at my chest and said, "You got big, BIG boobies. Huh, Mommy?"

"I guess I do. What about you? Do you have big boobies?"

"No, I have little, tiny ones," she said and my mother snickered.

"How about Shuggie, does she have big ones or tiny ones?"

Aubrey twisted her mouth sideways and stuck her finger in the air. "She has big boobies . . . AND really old ones."

So I was worried the next morning when we continued to see an older woman twisting through a particularly long line. The woman was probably in her seventies and was very well dressed. She was wearing a pair of khaki capri pants and a white sweater set with royal blue anchors stitched all over it. Her jewelry, her watch, and her hair all looked expensive. But this woman had either never outgrown her hippie-chick phase or she was experiencing the first signs of dementia because she was not wearing a bra.

Her sweater was knit cotton and clingy, and I could see her nipples clearly. Right above the waistband of her pants. If I could see them, I knew Aubrey could see them, and while I have the self-control and the wisdom to keep my mouth shut (most of the time), my four-year-old does not. Each boob looked like a sad, deflated balloon under that sweater. I caught Aubrey eyeing the woman's breasts as we passed her every three to five minutes and wasn't the least bit surprised when Aubrey whispered in my ear, "Momma, her forgot her booby bra and her boobies are so sad!" I was, however, quite thankful Aubrey had addressed me and not the woman in question.

Why would you go to the trouble to get dressed, put on makeup, and go somewhere if you can't be bothered to wear a bra? I can only assume that since these people could afford to be in Disney World that they could also afford undergarments. Or are we to take from this that Granny was pulling a Britney under her capri pants? (Ew.) Therefore, I further deduced that because half the women in the Magic Kingdom were not wearing bras, it was by their own choice.

This perplexed me a great deal. I, for one, am not opposed to or offended by the human body. I have breastfed all three of my children. (I said I hated it. That doesn't mean I didn't do it.) Even though I was always extremely uncomfortable whipping out the Big Berthas anywhere but my own home, I'm an advocate for women's right to breastfeed in public. (Discreetly, people!)

As a former ER nurse, I've seen more naked people than a "working girl" on the Vegas strip. I just couldn't understand wearing clothes without undergarments. I mean, what was the point of even putting a shirt on if I can see everything anyway? If you are going to go all *National Geographic,* I say take it all the way and just show up at Disney World wearing a thong made out of rope.

After spending every second standing in line at Disney World scrutinizing the Boobs of the World, I decided that something drastic must have happened to these women. Something life changing . . . something that would cause them to lose all faith that Victoria could be trusted with their secrets. Considering my last trip to Victoria's Secret, I had a pretty good idea what had happened to these women. They had met Skinny Big Boobs. The Victoria's Secret associate who didn't quite make the catalog.

After meeting Skinny myself, I guess I can see how some women have just decided that enough is freakin' enough and to revolt against bras altogether. God knows I thought about it as I ran out of the dressing room that fateful day.

I had finally finished breastfeeding Emma, after eleven long months, and I was tired of maternity and nursing bras. I had birthed two babies in less than two years, and I was ready to look like a woman again instead of a dairy cow. I wanted to shed my lactating image and buy myself something fun and flirty. I had my husband's credit card, and I wasn't afraid to use it. Zeb knew I was buying lingerie, so he didn't even warn me not to spend too much. I waltzed into the store with a smile on my face as I prepared for my comeback.

"Welcome to Victoria's Secret. My name is Skinny Big Boobs. Let me know if I can help you find a size."

"Actually, you may be able to help me. I've just finished breast-feeding, and I'm not really sure what size I am. Could you measure me?" I asked. I watched *Oprah*, and I knew that lots of women didn't even bother to get measured.

Skinny Big Boobs waltzed into my dressing room, measured my bosom, still ample despite ten months of Spinning classes and weight training, and left to gather some bras for me to try on.

"Here you go, sweetie. Try these on and let me know what

works," Skinny said as she shoved a handful of push-ups, demi-lace, and gravity-defying bras at me.

I struggled into the first bra and examined myself in the mirror. I tried to remember everything Oprah's bra expert had said on the show. The bra was uncomfortable—but were the cups too small or was the chest too tight? I sighed in disgust and wrestled my extra appendages into the next bra.

Crap—or was it the same bra I just had on? All the bras Skinny Big Boobs had brought me were the same color, and I hadn't been paying much attention. I continued staring at myself in the mirror and at the mounds of limp flesh where my full, perky boobs used to be. This was really getting depressing.

"How are we doing in there?" Skinny practically sang across the top of the dressing room door.

"Um, well, okay I guess. I'm not sure . . . are these all the same bra? I can't tell what the difference is."

"Why don't you open up and let me take a look?"

Uh, lemme think . . . because you're skinny and I'm fat and your boobs defy gravity and mine don't? I rolled my eyes in the mirror and opened the door.

"Let's see," Skinny said as she groped, poked, prodded, and pushed to try to make the lumps on my chest stand at attention. "Hmmm. Hm. Hmmm."

I frowned as I followed her gaze to my right breast and looked up at her quizzically. What the hell was she looking at?

"Oh, honey, it's okay. It's nothing to be ashamed of. You know, lots of women have one breast that is larger than the other."

"I don't . . ." I started to defend Righty, when I realized Skinny was correct. Dammit, Skinny Big Boobs had just called me out for being lopsided.

"You know," she continued, handing me another bra, "you

might try on one of these bras without padding. It might help mask your problem area."

I snatched the bra out of her hand and closed the door to the dressing room. I threw her stupid problem-masking bra on the ground and put my own bra and clothes back on. All I wanted was a bra that didn't scream, "MILK ME!" Something I could feel good about myself in. And that skank thinks she can come in here with her surgically proportioned breasts and judge me! I don't think so.

I huffed out of the dressing room and didn't even bother putting any of the bras back on their hangers. That'll teach her. If I'm going to pay good money for a sexy bra, I'd rather spend my money at Wal-Mart. At least there they charge what a bra is worth and I won't have to worry about anyone "helping" me.

So I could sort of understand the women of the world uniting in rebellion against bras and Skinny Big Boobs everywhere. If you just quit wearing bras altogether, you can not only avoid Skinny but also probably reduce your boob-sweat production.

Boob sweat, as I have mentioned when detailing for you all the reasons I hate breastfeeding, is one of the most disgusting things in the entire world. Something about smashing those melons together in a supportive bra (FYI: the more supportive, the less breathable the fabric, which leads to more boob sweat) causes the most atrocious sour smell on God's green earth; a hint of goat cheese gone bad with a nice vinegary finish. Ahhhh! (Not quite as sweet-smelling as Johnson's Baby Lotion, which is the best smell on the planet. I get lightheaded from huffing my kids after bath time. Seriously, it's as dangerous as paint fumes; I almost blacked out once.)

As a first-time mommy, I could not bear the thought of feeding my baby from what amounted to a human garbage dump. I would actually take two to three showers a day so Aubrey wouldn't have to be exposed to my boob sweat. With my second child, I didn't always have the time to shower every day and would sometimes feed her in the parking lot of the gym after a Spinning class. And the third one—bless Sadie's tiny little heart—I've all but nursed her while doing step aerobics. More than once, Sadie has gotten a bath only because her oldest sister was cuddling and loving on her and, after leaning in to smooch on Sadie's neck rolls, exclaimed, "Uggggh! Momma, WHAT is that SMELL? Her smells like SCHEESE!" (When your four-year-old starts complaining that your baby smells like goat cheese, you know the boob sweat has gotten out of control.)

As my momma says, I come from a long line of "L-M-N-O-P cups." Momma used to have some may-jah knockers, but she had the good sense to get those things downsized a few years back, and she's glad for it. My great-grandmother had Big Berthas so huge that she had a breast reduction before they even bothered to sew your nipples back on. I'm not kidding, people. My momma says they just lopped the ends right off.

I have been looking forward to getting downsized myself since I used my babysitting money to buy my first minimizer. Now that I've had my babies and breastfed them until my nipples gracefully touch my toes, I am ready to sign on the dotted line and return to Victoria's good graces . . . as long as Skinny Big Boobs doesn't offer to "help."

6

. . . .

Gettin' Your Fitness On

Trying to get back in shape after having a baby isn't near as fun as it sounds. I personally only like exercising once I'm leaving the gym with a smoothie in my hand. But I'd rather be somewhat thin and miserable while exercising than fat and miserable every day, so I exercise. After having Emma, my second child in twenty-two months, I put the pedal to the metal and lost my baby weight plus a little extra padding I had been carrying around since college. I worked with a fitness instructor and kept food logs. I went to the gym five or six days a week every week. I looked good, but I felt even better. It felt so good to have to buy new clothes because even my "skinny jeans" were too big.

Right before I got pregnant with my third child, we moved from Savannah, Georgia, to Charleston, South Carolina. I joined a gym the first week we were there. I didn't want to give myself the opportunity to backslide. My self-confidence was at an all-time high. I had two sweet, healthy babies, my husband's career had taken off, and I was able to quit my job to stay at home with my girls and could wear the same size clothes I wore in high school. Life was good.

I was flying high, until I walked into the gym one morning for a Body Pump class. I got all my equipment together and was admiring myself in the floor-length mirrors, not too conspicuously of course, just thinking how fabulous I looked and how hard I had worked to lose almost forty pounds—when the fitness instructor sauntered up to me, leaned in, and whispered with a cute little wink, "Did I see a little baby bump?"

Lord, help me. Lord, help her. I felt all the blood rush out of my face, and I stared at her in shock.

Was she raised by wolves? Did her momma not tell her that you never ask a woman if she's pregnant? I don't care if the baby's head is hanging out: you never ask a woman if she's pregnant! Play dumb and say, "Hmmm, Gina. Now, something is different about you. Wait, don't tell me! WHAT is it?" I don't care if she's screaming at the top of her lungs, "I NEED TO PUSH!" You'd be wise to keep up your Jessica Simpson act and say, "I know exactly what it is! You've lost weight!" When she screams, "I'm pregnant, YOU IDIOT!!" then and only then is it permissible for you to say, "I thought I saw a little baby bump." (And quite possibly not even then.)

I looked that skinny little tramp straight in her eye and said, "NO, as a matter of fact, you didn't! But thank you SO much for asking!" She gasped, and her twelve-pack and toned thighs took a step back. I couldn't decide whether to throw my Reebok step bench at her head or stay in the class and glare at her for an hour to punish her.

I ended up staying in class partly to punish the little wench and partly because just getting to the gym with two toddlers is such an inconvenience. You have to pack everything your kids may possibly need or want for the hour you will be exercising. You also get the pleasure of discussing every grunt and/or nuance your children might have and interpret these communications to a nursery worker who can't quit texting her boyfriend long enough to pay attention anyway.

On one of my first visits to the gym after our move to South Carolina, I took Emma, then around eighteen months, to the nursery. I hopped on the treadmill and started to sprint . . . okay, jog. I was five miles into my run . . . fine, one mile, when the nursery worker came out to tell me Emma had a dirty diaper.

"Her diaper bag has her name on it," I said as I gasped for the extra oxygen I needed to keep my pace and talk.

"Oh, we don't change diapers."

I stopped so abruptly on the treadmill that I was almost flung across the cardio room.

"I'm sorry. You what?"

"We're not supposed to change diapers."

I had to get off the treadmill to change my child's diaper. My child, who had just stopped crying for the first time since I had left the room. She clung to my leg and screamed as I tried unsuccessfully to extricate myself to finish my run. Wouldn't it just have been easier on everyone for the nursery worker to change the diaper?

"What exactly are these people getting paid for?" I wondered. Shouldn't they change the sign from CHILDCARE to WE'RE JUST GOING TO MAKE SURE NO ONE DIES WHILE YOU ARE EXERCISING? This is something I would like to have known before I signed a contract that included "childcare." Seriously, half the reason moms go to the gym is so someone else will take care of our kids for a couple of hours and we don't end up in a padded cell or on the eleven o'clock news!

For this and many other reasons, I have purchased hand weights and an exercise ball to exercise at home when it's too much trouble to leave the house. I prefer to go to the gym; I need someone yelling at me to work harder. Left to my own devices, I would stop at the first beads of sweat, pat myself on the back, say "good workout," and head to the juice bar.

A few weeks later, I got the weights out and started to workout. Aubrey was four years old at the time, and her partner in crime, Emma, was two. Both of them jumped right in with me. As we started doing sit-ups, Aubrey said, "Look, Momma, it's easier if you do this" and propped her elbows up on the floor underneath her.

I laughed. "Yeah, but that's cheating. You can't use your hands."

Aubrey glanced at me, then put her hands under her head mimicking me. After about two more crunches, Aubrey said, "But Momma, this HURTS my tummy. Can we stop now?" It sounded like somebody was ready to hit the juice bar.

I have taken a firm stand against exercising when pregnant for several reasons. The first and most important being that I had horrendous morning sickness with all three pregnancies. I was sick all day long, every day, for months. This is no way to exercise, and if you lose ten pounds in your first trimester from vomiting, you probably don't need to be working out anyway. Plus, it was hard to find the motivation to go to the gym when, no matter what I did, I was gaining weight.

After giving birth to Sadie, my third daughter in four years, I was perfectly happy to be fat for a few months while I finished breastfeeding, until I got a card in the mail from my little brother's fiancée. I called my sister Blair immediately and said, "Did you get a card in the mail from Anna?"

She could tell by the tone of my voice that I was panicking, so she said, "OH NO! They didn't break up, did they?"

"Oh no, it's so much worse than that . . ."

"Aw crap, did she ask us to be in the wedding?"

"Yep."

I was flattered she asked me, but I was horrified. I could wear a sarong at the pool all summer but would probably look suspicious walking down the aisle that way.

I reluctantly started going back to the gym, and Blair started doing Weight Watchers. My feelings about exercising when breastfeeding are about the same as they are when pregnant: it's pointless. When I'm pregnant I'm going to gain weight no matter what. When nursing, my body fights to hold on to fat like I'm going to be hibernating. For example, my sister lost nine pounds in two weeks on Weight Watchers; I, on the other hand, gained a pound and a half going to the gym for a week. (Please save the muscle-weighs-more-than-fat tirade for someone else. When I exercise while breastfeeding, I am ravenous and will eat anything in sight. I end up consuming more calories than I burn.)

As summer quickly approached, I finally had to break down and buy a bathing suit. No amount of tugging and/or lubricant could coax my postbaby body into one of the million suits I already owned. There was no way my baby's meal tickets were going to be squeezed into anything I already had.

I went to Target (also known to mommies across the country as their "happy place") and bought a "Big Girra Bathing Suit."

"Mommy, how 'bout this one? It is SO cute!" Aubrey said as she picked up a hot-pink string bikini.

I looked critically at the bathing suit she was holding and quickly deduced that the triangle top probably wouldn't even cover my zipple.

"No, baby. I don't want the other mommies at the pool to have nightmares."

We continued back to the "women's sizes," and I flattered myself with the first size I chose and forced it onto my body. Lycra snapped and crackled as I pulled, stretched, and sucked in. After seeing my reflection closely resembled an Italian sausage I'd eaten once, I was forced to get a larger size.

This should have meant that I took off the suit and put my clothes back on to go get another one. But if you're shopping for clothes at a place where you can also buy an ICEE or a foot-long hot dog, you need to realize that no one is going to come knock softly on your door to see if you need another size. I'm lazy, though, so I put on the swimsuit cover-up I was trying on and walked to get another size, dressed for the pool.

I'm not going to tell you what size I ended up in, though I will say it had a *W* behind the numbers. (Plural. As in there was more than one.) I called my sister while I was checking out, and she texted back, "I'm in WW's [Weight Watchers] can't talk, ttyl :)."

I texted her back, "How many pts are a Butterfinger & a Coke cuz that's what I'm eating rite now?" Maybe I can convince Anna that all of the bridesmaids should be in sarongs.

7

. . . .

Biscuit-Dough Boobies

I believe I have adequately described how much I hate my boobies. They were large and in charge before I was ever pregnant, but after three pregnancies in four years and breastfeeding all three babies for varied lengths of time, I had shot the elastic in my boobs like a fat girl in a cheap pair of pantyhose. My breasts were not only ginormous, but they hung almost to my waistline, à la *National Geographic,* covering my rib cage entirely.

There has never been a time in my life when I had small boobs. I'm pretty sure I wore a sports bra under my onesies as a baby. My younger sister came to visit me shortly after her first child and my third child were born. We were eating ice cream directly out of the carton and discussing our boobs as only sisters can.

"Before I had Tucker, I could see underneath my boobs," she said, staring off into the distance with a dreamy look in her eyes.

"Huh?"

"Under my boobs . . . like when I looked in the mirror, I could SEE underneath my boobs. Now they sag, and they feel so gross."

"Canned biscuit dough," I said matter-of-factly as I took another bite of ice cream. "My friend Kasey says post-baby boobs are the consistency of canned biscuit dough, and she's right. I can't remember being able to see my rib cage much less the underside of my boobs. You're still perky compared to me, so quit whining."

Because I was finally finished having babies, it was time. Time for me to make an appointment I'd been waiting to make since high school—it was time to call the plastic surgeon. I discussed having a breast reduction with my husband, and while Zeb was very supportive of whatever I wanted to do, he continued to insist that they weren't "that" big. I'm not exactly sure what "that" was, but I knew that it was time to put the Big Berthas out of their misery. They had served our family well, but it was time to trade them in for some Itsy Bitsy Betsies.

I made the appointment and counted down the days until my consultation. Before I knew it, Zeb and I were sitting on a love seat in the surgeon's office, answering questions about my medical history and ogling before and after pictures of the doctor's other patients. Actually, I ogled and Zeb slept. He had been up with the baby the night before and was so tired that even looking at bare boobies didn't interest him.

"Oh, honey! Look at those! They are so cute and perky!" I said.

Zeb opened his eyes, wiped the drool off of his chin, and tried to look interested.

"What size bra are you in now?" the nurse asked as the doctor walked in the room.

"A 38F," I answered.

I saw the skepticism on their faces as they checked out my chest and looked at each other, but they didn't comment as they escorted me to an exam room.

I was more than a little nervous about "letting down my boobs" in front of complete and perfect strangers, even if they were medical professionals. At least when I go to the ob-gyn for a breast exam, I'm lying on my back and my boobs have some semblance of being round and, well, boob-shaped. Being horizontal also gives the false impression they are located north of my waistband. I was about to be standing up, totally vertical, so they could get the full effect of gravity on my boobalas. And in addition, I would be posing for topless pictures for the first time in my life. (Xanax, anyone?)

I'm no good at nervous small talk. I tend to get diarrhea of the mouth when I am nervous, and it never ends well. After enlisting my husband's help in putting on a paper gown the size of one of Britney Spears's bikini tops, I perched on the exam table and waited for the doctor with my zipples hanging out from the bottom of the gown.

The doctor and his nurse entered the room; he sat on his stool, rolled over in front of me, and said, "All right, let's see what we've got."

I took a deep breath, closed my eyes, and opened the gown.

"WOW! That's really surprising. I mean, I wasn't expecting that at all. You are so small-framed. You hide them really well."

I shot Zeb a look and whispered, "SEE! They are that big!" I laughed nervously. The doctor began measuring and quietly dictating into a handheld tape recorder.

"Yeah, that's the reaction I always get . . . ," I said as I began my monologue. "I mean, not that I show them to a lot of people . . . or

ANYONE. I mean, I don't usually show them to anyone . . . but when I say I want to have a breast reduction, people are always like, 'Why?' But I don't show them to anybody . . . like my husband and my doctor are the only ones that have ever seen them. Well, of course, except for my kids . . . and my mom. And I guess my sister and, well, probably more people than that because I DID breastfeed, but I always tried to be discreet, but you know sometimes the blanket would slip, so I may have flashed a few people, but it was totally an accident." (Shut up, shut up, SHUT UP, Robin! The less you talk, the faster you can get dressed!) "I'm uh, I'm going to stop talking now . . . sorry. Sorry. I do this when I'm nervous."

As the doctor finished his exam, Zeb yawned in his corner and rolled his eyes at me, or maybe he was just going back to sleep. The doctor discussed the procedure, risks, and postoperative care and asked if we had any questions before he left the room. I dressed as quickly as possible and asked Zeb, "So? What do you think?"

"His sock was on inside out."

"What? Are you still asleep? I'm getting new boobs, and all you have to say is, 'His sock is inside out'?"

He shrugged and yawned as we walked out of the exam room to schedule my surgery.

The months until my surgery flew by, and I struggled with what to tell my children. I wanted them to understand why I wouldn't be able to pick them up and carry them around for a while, but I didn't want to scare them or tell them too soon so that they would spend days or weeks worrying.

My mother was coming to help me take care of the house and the kids while I recovered, so two days before my surgery I decided to talk to Aubrey. I picked her up from school one afternoon, and as we drove home I said, "Shuggie is going to be here in two days!"

"Woo-hoooo!" Aubrey squealed and clapped her hands.

"Shuggie is going to come and help us because Mommy is going to have an operation."

"What's an op-er-a-tion?"

"Well, I'm going to go to the hospital, and the doctor is going to fix my boobies, because they are really big and they make my neck and my back hurt."

"Ooooo, can I watch?" she asked excitedly.

"NO! You can't watch!"

"Please, Momma! Please, please, please! I won't touch anyfing, I promise!"

I sighed. As always, my point was completely lost on my audience—at least she wasn't freaked out by the idea or hadn't asked how, exactly, my boobs were going to become smaller.

Later that evening, I was spooning Aubrey in her bed, reading a book with her. She was leaning backward, trying to snuggle closer to me, when she looked up at me, totally exasperated, and said, "MOM. Your booby is totally blocking me!"

"Oh, sorry," I said as I reached over and hitched one of the Berthas out of her way.

Aubrey snuggled closer to me and asked, "Is that why you are getting your boobies shorter, Mommy?"

Maybe she hadn't missed my point after all.

Your Husband: Your Helpmate
and Your Mortal Enemy

One of the hardest things I have discovered about being a mother is dividing my time between my husband and my children. I never anticipated this problem in the seven years we were married B.C. (Before Children). We liked each other. We loved each other. We probably even luv'd each other. We enjoyed spending time together, going to a movie on the spur of the moment, taking a spontaneous ride on our Harley, going to Auburn football games, and working in our garden. (He worked and I tanned, but whatever.) It was as close to marital bliss as I believe is realistically possible.

When our first child was born, it was like someone had dropped an atomic bomb in the middle of our little relationship utopia. We could no longer go for long rides through the back roads of Lee County on our Harley. For one thing, there was nowhere to strap the car seat, and for another, I was an ER nurse and was terrified that something would happen to me or my husband on the bike and that our child would be orphaned.

We could no longer spend all day Saturday tailgating with friends, standing out in the hot Auburn sun waiting for kickoff. We couldn't even go to a movie without planning ahead, getting a babysitter, and describing in depth everything our baby might possibly want or need in the two hours we would be gone.

Date nights are important, but they can also be expensive and a lot of trouble. As moms and dads, you are already exhausted from working, school, and the responsibilities of life. Very often it's easier to stay in your sweatpants and order a pizza instead of going through all the effort and expense it takes to actually get all dressed up to leave your house and go somewhere. Many parents give up the fight for date night, and, slowly, Mom becomes so wrapped up in the kids and Dad becomes so wrapped up in *Sports Center* that their LUV relationship begins to fade into the background. You need to have a good and loving relationship with your spouse.

The most important reason you need to invest in a relationship with your husband is so you don't end up in the state penitentiary doing ten to twenty-five hard years for involuntary manslaughter, once you've seen all the asinine things he's going to do to your kid.

There are several areas where you are liable to butt heads with your otherwise intelligent husband. I discovered that not only was my husband completely and totally color-blind, he also had some sort of visual disturbance that prevented him from being able to distinguish different patterns, i.e., polka dots from flowers or stripes. This was evidenced every single time he dressed our child, which happened on a pretty regular basis since I was working full-time in the ER as a nurse when she was born and he was working on his master's degree.

I can tell you this for a scientific fact: men do not hear as well as women. I have to sleep with earplugs to keep from hearing every snort, grunt, and shifting of blankets that come from the nursery. Every sound your baby makes in the middle of the night is a potential emergency. Since Aubrey's birth, I have had Mommy Post-Traumatic Stress Disorder. Every time I lie down to sleep and somebody makes a noise, every nerve in my body jumps. It's a jolt of adrenaline and electricity that makes my fingertips and toes twitch. I sit straight up in bed, unhook my nursing bra, and scream, "WHO'S HUNGRY?!" My husband, on the other hand, has slept through innumerable middle-of-the-night tantrums thrown by screaming, crying, inconsolable babies without ever stirring.

When Aubrey was three months old, I came home from a twelve-hour shift in the ER at 11:30 P.M. to find her screaming bloody murder. I picked her up and ran through the house with my heart racing, thinking my husband must be hurt. Someone must have broken into the house and attacked him, and I would find him sprawled on the floor. Or maybe he was sick, doubled over the toilet with some highly contagious and deathly strain of a stomach bug or . . . I skidded around the corner into our bedroom and found him—asleep. He was actually sleeping while our child screamed. He was out cold, with the baby monitor at full volume.

From that point on, he had to put her in the bed with him to go to sleep, and I would put her in her own bed when I came home. I found them on more than one occasion cuddled up in the bed with Daddy fast asleep and Aubrey looking at me like, "Poor little guy, he was all tuckered out."

Once we transitioned Aubrey from the baby bed to the big-girl bed, we had a whole new set of problems. My husband had been officially relieved from night duty with our kids when I heard him saying in the middle of the night to Aubrey, who was six weeks old, "WHAT is wrong with you??? Stop crying and just tell me what you want!" Her continued crying and his continued sensitivity weren't exactly compatible with Mommy getting a full night's sleep, so we developed day and night shifts and stuck to that schedule until Emma, our second child, came along.

Emma threw a slight kink in our system because on many nights I would get one child down just as the other was waking up. On nights that both girls were up, I would deal with Emma, since I was breastfeeding, and Zeb would take care of getting Aubrey back to bed.

I was making Aubrey's bed one morning and found a piece of petrified string cheese.

"Hmmm," I thought to myself. "How in the world did that get there?"

When Zeb came home from work that evening, I casually said, "I found an old piece of string cheese in Aubrey's bed today."

"Oh, she woke up the other night and said she was hungry. She wanted string cheese, so I gave her some and put her back in the bed."

"YOU DID WHAT?!"

"I gave her some string cheese. She said she was hungry."

"Are you kidding me? You gave a two-year-old string cheese and put her in the bed with it! What were you thinking? She could have choked to death! She only said she was hungry as a stalling tactic! And guess what? Now she KNOWS you are a SUCKER, and now she's going to come back for more! DON'T you EVER give my baby food and put her in the bed with it! YOU are going to fix this! Do you hear me? Don't be waking me up in the middle of the night when she comes begging you for more cheese!"

Thus began the weeklong cheese fiasco. Every night around two in the morning, Aubrey would creep into our room, slip over to Zeb's side of the bed, and wail for string cheese. He would get up and put her back in the bed, minus the cheese. He was learning his lesson the hard way, or so I thought.

A couple of weeks passed, and I was beginning to think the cheese fiasco was over. I was up before daylight one morning nursing Emma, when Aubrey came walking sideways into our living room and pointing to her back.

"Wook, Momma, wook." She continued to point.

There on her Elmo pajamas was a piece of string cheese that had melted with her body heat into a circle the size of a personal pan pizza. I took her shirt off and began the arduous process of scraping the cheese off her favorite pajamas without putting a hole in them.

I called Zeb. "Dude. You are so busted." I didn't need to say anything else on the matter. The cheese fiasco was finally over.

Road trips are another great time to bond with your husband. We have always lived hundreds of miles away from our extended families in Alabama. We are used to loading up everything we own and taking road trips with our kids. Zeb usually drives, reluctantly I might add, while I spend most of my time turned around backward tending to the kids, passing out snacks, and picking up whatever toys they have dropped.

Usually somewhere along our route to Alabama, I will glance at Aubrey and notice that she is asleep with the DVD still running.

"Zeb, is Emma asleep?" I'll whisper to him.

"How am I supposed to know?" he'll say. "I'm driving."

"ZEB, look in the rearview mirror OR pretend you are checking your blind spot and GLANCE at her to see if she is asleep."

"That's really not safe, Robin."

Is he serious? Does he realize that I drive with them in the car every day and can keep one hand on the wheel and my eyes on the road and still reach their baby dolls in the backseat when they drop them?

"LOOK AT HER!" I'll hiss at him.

"Yeah, she's asleep."

I turn the DVD player off and slam it shut.

When we made the move from Savannah, Georgia, to Mount Pleasant, South Carolina, in November 2007, he was driving his car and pulling a trailer with his motorcycle. Because my car has the DVD player, I had eighteen-month-old Emma and three-year-old Aubrey in the car with me. We got into Charleston around dark, and as we were crossing the Ravenel Bridge, my cell phone rang. It was Zeb.

"Did you see that battleship?!" He began to describe the USS *Yorktown* in vivid detail.

"What battleship?" I asked him.

"The one we are driving over."

Smoke began to pour out of my ears, and my blood began to boil. I could feel my chest tightening as my blood pressure rose. "I'm SORRY! You mean the one that is five hundred feet BE-LOW us and a quarter of a mile BEHIND us? Are you for real? You are pulling a trailer, talking on your cell phone, and driving across a six-lane bridge you've never driven on before IN THE DARK, and you aren't capable of looking in the backseat to see if your child is sleeping?" I hung up the phone.

The next time we were in the car headed to Alabama and things got quiet, I asked, "Is Emma sleeping?"

"I don't know," he said. "I'm driving."

I was quick to reply. "Just pretend she's a battleship."

No matter how idiotic your husband's behavior is with or in front of your kids, you married him. So you have to deal with it, and you'd better be careful how. Zeb called one Sunday to tell me he was on his way home from work. I hung up the phone and turned to the girls. "Daddy's on his way home from work!" I knew they would be excited to see him because he had worked all weekend. A few minutes passed, and Aubrey said angrily, "Why you call my daddy a jerk, Momma?"

"Which time?" I thought to myself as I scrambled to try to figure out what she was referring to. It finally hit me, and I exclaimed, "I didn't call Daddy a JERK. I said he's on his way home from WORK!"

Aubrey looked at me with scorn and said, "I don't fink so!"

I have to admit that I married the perfect man, though. He is a man's man but ended up with three daughters. He can fix anything, which is nice because I break just about everything. In exchange for my staying up late with whichever child isn't cooperating, he lets me sleep late every Saturday and Sunday and has never complained about it. (He is mine, and you can't have him and, yes, I would take my earrings off and fight for him.) He washes dishes or the kids every night after dinner. And he lets me pick which of those chores I'd rather do, which means that most nights I end up cleaning the kitchen and sipping on some Mommy Juice (read: whatever brand of wine was on sale at Wal-Mart this particular week) while he bathes the girls, brushes teeth, brushes "knobs" out of hair, and reads the girls a story before bed. He works up to fourteen hours a day some days and comes home exhausted but willing to do anything I ask of him. Not only can he change my oil and build an exact replica of the Pottery Barn bookcase I've been eyeing, but he can also give a mean pedicure. He (thanks to extensive training from his mother and three sisters) has learned that when a girl cries, it's not always for a reason and that the appropriate response is always a hug and an apology. His only fault is that he is a man and doesn't do things the way I would.

Ah, well. I guess nobody is perfect.

The Shirt Off My Back

One thing I know for sure is that you can never appreciate the sacrifices that your mother made for you until you are a mother yourself and realize what an ungrateful little jerk you were. Even as a young adult, when you start to realize that your mother isn't the complete idiot you thought she was during your teen years, you still don't really get it.

True understanding comes when you are sitting on the toilet at two o'clock in the morning, four days after having a baby, experiencing diarrhea and attempting to still breastfeed your child because your husband is asleep and there is no one else to take up the slack. You are now the momma. You are now in charge. You start to think about all those years you were able to go to sleep whenever you wanted to, without a thought as to who would clean up the mess in the kitchen or if everybody in the house had clean clothes to wear the next day. You begin to see that while you were lying in bed reading the latest Babysitters

Club book, your mother was working her butt off for your un-grateful, smart-mouthed self. And now it's your turn.

Once you are somebody's momma, you begin to learn the meaning of the word "sacrifice." Some sacrifices are made simply to shut your children up. These sacrifices have few nega-tive results for the mother and produce a quick and convenient stop to a tantrum in progress.

When I was a little girl and my mother would go out of town or even out for the night and I was really missing her, I would go in her closet and steal a nightgown to snuggle with. Being able to hold on to something of hers, something that smelled like her, was so comforting. The only thing I can think of to this day that smells better than my mother is my babies after bath time. And if my mom has been holding one of my babies and they get the Shuggie/baby combo going, I'm likely to sniff them until I get light-headed or my husband tells me to stop because people are staring.

When Emma was two years old, she didn't feel well and had trouble sleeping through the night. One night, she came in our bedroom and wanted to crawl in the bed with us. She thrashes violently in her sleep, so in order for Zeb and me to get any rest, she had to go back to her bed. She was crying for me as Zeb was picking her up to carry her to her room.

"Emma, you want to sleep with Mommy's shirt?" I asked her.

"Yeah, I do, Mommy. I do!"

I snatched my shirt off, threw it to Zeb, and went back to sleep in my sports bra.

A few nights later, Emma was still running a fever and wanted to sleep in our bed again.

"Pweeeeeze, Mommy! Can I sweep in you bed? I be weally, weally still and a good gull. I will, Momma!"

"Emma, I already said no. But I'll lay down in your bed with you for a little while, okay?" Zeb told her as he scooped her up and carried her to bed.

After nursing the baby, I went into the big girls' room to let Zeb know I was getting in the shower.

"MOMMY! Daddy laid in Emma's bed and snuggled wif her and not wif me! It's NOT FAIR!" Aubrey cried.

I sighed as I lay down with Aubrey for a few minutes to console her.

"All right, give me a kiss, Aubrey." She puckered up and gave me a kiss as I tried to escape from their bedroom to hit the shower.

As I leaned over to kiss Emma, she started whining, "MOMMY! You laid down wis Aub-a-rey and not wis me! It not fair!"

Instead of banging my head against the wall until I lost consciousness, I asked Emma if she wanted to sleep with my shirt.

"Yeah, yeah, yeah . . . cober me up wit it, Momma," she said. I did, and my shirt covered her from head to toe.

"Why you give that to her, Momma?" Aubrey asked.

"I don't know, baby. She just likes it," I told Aubrey as I tucked her blanket around her tighter.

Aubrey began to giggle, "Wellllllllll, I like your pants."

I didn't even hesitate or stop to think about it. I wanted a shower and I wanted sleep, in that order. ASAP. I ripped my pajama pants off and threw them to her. The girls were shrieking with laughter. I was now standing in between their two beds in nothing but my bra and panties.

Emma said with a completely straight face, "Well, I wike you underwears, Momma . . ."

I fell on the floor I was laughing so hard. But a good mother

knows where to draw the line, and giving your child a pair of
dirty underwear to snuggle with definitely falls in the bad-mother
category.

"I don't know who y'all think you are or what you're playing
at, but that is IT! I'm drawing the line! You are NOT getting my
underwear OR my booby bra! GOOD NIGHT!" I could still
hear them cackling as I closed the door.

The daily sacrifices a mother makes are never-ending. You
skip breakfast to make lunches for your kids. You wanted the
last slice of pizza, but so did one of your kids, so you gave it up.
You were planning on having coffee with a friend and instead
end up at home because one of your kids isn't feeling well. Sick
kids stop everything in your house. Sick husbands stop the rota-
tion of the planets around the sun. But if Momma is sick? Nobody gives a crap.

When I was seven months pregnant with my third daughter,
Aubrey had a "performance" at her school. Of course, it wasn't
directly after school, which would mean I would already be
there in all of my pregnant glory. Nope, it was at 6:00 P.M. This
is the worst time of day for any mother of young children. Your
kids are tired, hungry, and whiny. So are you, but again, you are
the mother and nobody cares how you feel. You still have to
cook, feed everyone, clean the kitchen, bathe everyone, brush
their teeth, read them stories, and get them in the bed before
you are allowed to think about doing anything for yourself.

Lots of moms refer to this time of day as "the witching
hour." I call it "happy hour" only because that's when I break
out the Mommy Juice. Y'all don't worry about me drinking too
much. I drink wine like I drink coffee—when my kids let me. I
normally get down about half a glass before I end up getting
sucked into reading a story or refereeing a fight. On this day in

particular, no one in my house was happy. Especially me, because I was knocked up and couldn't even have a glass of wine.

Aubrey's very first school performance was smack dab in the middle of "happy hour," and even though I was seven months pregnant and taking medication to keep from having contractions, which also caused my hands to shake and my heart to race, nobody cared. We had to go to her performance. Happy hour is bad even on a good day. But when you have to get everyone in your house not just dressed, but dressed in church clothes, with clean faces, and fed before 5:30, it's not going to be pretty. And it wasn't, but somehow we pulled it off.

Aubrey had been practicing her songs all week, and her little face would just beam at me as she belted out the words to "God Is So Good." We had the camera and the video camera and were ready to document this recital for posterity.

We got to the school and waddled into the auditorium (I waddled and everybody else pretty much just walked, but you get the idea). Zeb looked around and found the most strategic spot for us to sit so that he could get a good camera angle. I made sure the lens cap was off of my camera and the power was on. Then there she was ... my sweet Aubrey, marching down the aisle in her Sunday finest, chest puffed out, curls bouncing, and grinning from ear to ear. All the stress of getting there just melted away. That was my baby, the cutest, sweetest, and probably the smartest child on that whole stage. I wanted to elbow the mom beside me and let her know which one was mine. Thank God, I restrained myself.

The choir director stood in front of them, the music began, and all fifty children started singing about the goodness of God. All but one and that would be mine. My child stood on the stage, picked her nose, and ate her boogers in front of the entire auditorium for the duration of the song. She didn't sing a single note. I have it on video; I can prove it. I was horrified. I really thought our booger-picking days were over after Mrs. Emily taught Aubrey's class about germs during the letter *G* week. Apparently the stress of being in front of all those people was more than my child could bear, and under the pressure she just crumbled and regressed.

After the performance, my husband and I went to get Aubrey from her classroom.

"Momma! Daddy! Did you see me?"

"Oh, yes. We saw you! You did such a great job! Mommy and Daddy are SOOOO proud of you," I gushed.

While I was thinking, "I cannot believe that I put on a bra, makeup, and REAL clothes just to come and watch you eat boogers for five minutes!" she was totally oblivious to what she had done. A good mother knows not only when to sacrifice for her children but also when and where to lie to them.

Some sacrifices are only temporary. My kids inherited their horrendous morning-time disposition from me. So I understand when they wake up grouchy or cry because someone is looking at them. I get it. I feel that way, too.

One afternoon, Aubrey woke up from her nap, screaming, crying, wallowing on the floor, and just generally acting a fool. "Aha," I thought, "she needs food." She screamed something about a peanut butter and jelly sandwich in the midst of her writhing fit. I was on it. Even though I had a headache, was dying of thirst, not wearing any pants (I was jerked out of the bed by my two-year-old and not allowed to dress), and realized the only thing I'd eaten all day long was half a chicken salad sandwich—on the heel, gross—my baby was hungry and wanted a sandwich, and all that other stuff could wait. My headache, plus the need for water, ibuprofen, and pants—they would all have to be dealt with after I made a quick PB&J. I am a mother, a martyr; I would sacrifice for my children.

I made the sandwich, generous with the jelly and cut into squares. Just the way my baby likes it. And even though I knew she'd only eat half, I made her a whole sandwich because to do otherwise would be to insinuate that she is a "baby." Done.

"Here, baby, here's your sandwich."

"Thanks, Momma."

"Can I have one bite?"

Aubrey rolled her eyes, totally aggravated and annoyed with me. "Make your OWN sandwich."

As if she had just worked so hard to make that sandwich herself. The nerve of that child. But a good mother can recognize when a sacrifice is only temporary. I knew there was no way she'd eat the whole sandwich. In a matter of minutes, she would drop half on the floor and be on to something else. "Whatever," I muttered to myself. "I'll eat the other half once it ends up on the floor." At least I swept yesterday. That would cut down on miscellaneous debris that will get stuck to it when she drops it on the floor. I am after all, a mother, a martyr . . . I can sacrifice for my children.

10

. . . .

Ketchup Is a Vegetable

If you thought feeding your child was a chore when all you had to do was stick a bottle or a boob in his mouth, you are in for a fine surprise. Once you start feeding that child baby food, he's going to develop an opinion. Once he is old enough to really make some noise? He's going to let you and all your neighbors hear about it when you try to feed him spinach and sardines, or whichever flavor he has decided he hates that day. Unless you are feeding him a jarful of pureed candy corn, he's not going to like everything you put in his sweet little mouth.

Don't be getting all smug when your baby eats vegetables at first. You will pay. Do you hear me? It will bite you right in the butt. My oldest child went from eating anything I stuck in her mouth to refusing just about everything I fed her. For years. She got real particular, real fast. I tried talking to other moms about it, but I made a huge miscalculation and ended up talking to the Alpha Mom in Aubrey's preschool class. (You know the one.

She struggles just like you do, but she'll never give you the satisfaction of knowing it.)

We were having a Christmas party for their two-year-old class and one of the moms had brought a vegetable tray. Because, you know, nothing screams "party time" to a roomful of toddlers like raw broccoli and cherry tomatoes. I say if we're going to call this a party, give 'em pizza and cupcakes. Let's really turn this mutha out. But nobody asked me.

Alpha Mom's little boy was chowing down on the veggie tray. This kid was eating broccoli, carrots, cucumbers, and tomatoes. Raw. This was unprecedented toddler behavior. I was in awe.

I sidled up to his mom and whispered, "HOW do you get him to eat vegetables like that?"

I knew I had asked the wrong woman as soon as the words were out of my mouth. She all but had a sign on her forehead declaring, "I KNEW I WAS A BETTER MOTHER THAN YOU!" But it was too late. I had released my words into the universe, and now I had to listen to what this idiot had to say.

"Well," she began, with a smirk I wanted to knock off of her face, "I tell him that the cucumber slices are wagon wheels and the broccoli is little trees. He even eats green beans! I tell him they are green french fries, and he dips them in ketchup!" She smiled broadly. She was proud, of herself and her child.

"I wish my kid was that stupid, but unfortunately my child is smart enough to tell the difference between a green bean and a french fry," I thought to myself. And at my house, ketchup is a vegetable.

Alpha Mom wasn't near as smug at her child's birthday party a few weeks later. He was wearing a cast on his left leg and limping.

"What in the world happened to him?" I asked, truly concerned.

Alpha Mom flushed redder than a cherry tomato. Before she could speak, her mother-in-law quipped, "She run him over in the driveway." Oh. My. Lanta. I hope I never know that level of mommy guilt.

Rather than eat healthy, vitamin-enriched McNuggets, my own kids developed a love for nonfood items, such as sand, charcoal, ashes, and dirt. When Aubrey was eighteen months old, she ate ashes out of our fireplace and charcoal out of the grill on the same day (while her father was in charge of her, I might add). That's when I got online to do some research. She had to have some sort of pica disorder, a vitamin deficiency most common in pregnant women who crave and eat things like laundry detergent and dirt. But my search was in vain, and I couldn't find any information on an actual disorder.

While I asked Dr. Google, my husband stood over my shoulder saying, "Don't worry, it's good for her. It's like a vaccine."

I'm trying to avoid my child getting a tapeworm or some disgusting disease, and he thinks she's being vaccinated. Please.

I resorted to desperate measures to keep her from eating things that were not meant to be digested. I bought her an ice cream cone at the beach as an alternative to eating sand. When the child actually spit out ice cream to put more sand in her mouth, I realized I was defeated. There was just no helping a kid who would actually spit out cold and creamy ice cream on a hot day at the beach in order to eat sand. I could discourage her, but unless I wanted to spend the next year freaking out every time she put something in her mouth, I was going to have to relax. We lived ten minutes from the Atlantic Ocean—either I had to adjust or we had to stay in the house.

On our next day at the beach, I didn't really fight it. I would rinse her mouth out occasionally and say half-heartedly, "Hey, cut that out." But I knew in my heart she loved to eat sand, and if I didn't want her to do it, I had no business bringing her to the beach. I was about eight months pregnant with Emma at the time, propped up in a lounge chair, sipping on a bottle of water. Aubrey was digging happily in the sand and licking her fingers as my husband and I talked and enjoyed the day together.

"Excuse me, ma'am . . ." A young guy in his early twenties stopped walking on the beach to address me.

"Yes?" I replied, trying to ignore the "ma'am."

"Um, your kid is eating sand . . ." He looked at me like I was letting her play with razor blades.

"We're at the beach! What do you want me to do?!" I screamed at this perfect stranger.

He glanced at his friends, turned, and quickly walked away.

"Yeah, you KEEP walking!" I yelled after him.

Now, you are probably sitting there reading this and thinking, "Well, she needs to read one of those clever new cookbooks about how to hide veggies in her children's food." I have been there and done that, and my children can sniff out a sweet potato like a drug dog working border patrol. It doesn't work for me, but you go right ahead and steam your veggies, make purees, and mix them in your Kraft Easy Mac and just see what happens.

If getting your kids to eat is a hassle, you have no idea what's going to happen when you start trying to coordinate the sleep schedules of multiple people. Sleeping and eating are two of the most basic human functions, so you would think they would come naturally. And you would be wrong.

If sleep deprivation is a form of torture, the CIA needs to unleash my kids on all Al Qaeda suspects in captivity. They are professional nap-time terrorists who are very dedicated to their own little jihad. I'm pretty sure that they have a team meeting every morning while I'm sleeping for the measly thirty minutes they so graciously allow me every day.

In my head it goes something like this:

My oldest, Aubrey, functions as team leader and opens the meeting. "I know we ran out of Cheerios yesterday, so I'll scream and cry for the first two hours for Cheerios. Emma, you just eat whatever she gives you. Baby Sadie, you cry until she whips out a Big Bertha."

Middle child Emma throws in her two cents. "I wore my favorite dress yesterday and got ketchup ALL over it, and since Mommy hasn't done laundry in a week, I'll refuse to wear anything but that."

"Good thinking, Emma! Baby Sadie, you wait 'til we are ready to walk out the door to poop. You know how much Momma hates having to come back in the house once we're all in the car," Aubrey says with a maniacal laugh.

They cover every aspect of the day, filling out spreadsheets with sleeping schedules so I am never left unsupervised, and take turns being the "good one" to try to avoid arousing my suspicions. But I am onto them . . . I just can't find any evidence of premeditation.

Once during nap time, I went from bed to bed getting everyone settled in. After numerous threats, I finally got everyone including Sadie asleep. I went to climb into my bed with Aubrey and realized she was smack dab in the center of my "nest-o'-pillows" asleep—the nerve! But I was determined, so I grabbed a couple of extra pillows and got in the bed on the other side . . . and woke her up.

"I'll just close my eyes and she'll go back to sleep," I thought to myself.

Wrong.

She was awake and whining for juice. I dragged my butt out of the nice warm bed, got her juice, and told her that nap time was not over and to go back to sleep. But it was pointless; I should have realized it then and there. She had taken a power nap . . . the bane of every mother's existence.

For some unknown reason, maybe denial, I continued to lie in the bed and try to sleep. About every four minutes, just as my thoughts were getting cloudy and I was beginning to drift off, Aubrey would touch me—just enough to wake me up. Torture.

I rolled away from her and closed my eyes for the hundredth time. I was lying on a Polly Pocket, but it was a small price to pay if I could just sleep for thirty minutes . . . dammit, the Polly Pocket was really hurting. (They really had thought of everything.)

I rolled back toward Aubrey but kept my eyes slammed shut. I didn't want to give her any indication that I was awake. I could hear her moving around and knew she'd pounce at the slightest sign of weakness. All of a sudden I felt her lunge toward me, and my nostrils were covered by her mouth as she took a DEEEEEP breath and blew her orange-juice breath into my nostrils! I sat up, choking from the sudden and unexpected influx of air into my lungs.

What the hell was that? Did they talk about it at this morning's meeting? Who was the mastermind of this new technique?

As I got out of bed, defeated, I had another mental picture of their team meeting. White-blond curls bouncing, they leaned together in conspiracy, with six tiny hands in a circle. "Ready . . . BREAK!" I could just see Emma and Sadie saluting their commander as they commenced to driving me right over the edge.

11

· · · · · · ·

Road Trips

Traveling with kids is a joy in and of itself. There is nothing like packing up your entire house, shoving it all in your car, and sitting less than two feet away from every member of your immediate family for hours on end. The fun increases exponentially with each child you add to the mix. You have to pack everything you might possibly need. Clothes for all three kids, extra clothes for the two-year-old in case she has a potty accident, extra clothes for the baby in case she throws up, extra clothes for everybody for riding horses and four-wheelers on the farm. Diapers and wipes and Pull-Ups, snacks and juice cups and bottles. Coloring books, favorite stuffed animals, favorite blankies.

My husband, Zeb, who is just barely capable of packing everything he needs for a trip (like a suit when we went home for my sister's wedding), likes to preface every road trip with this statement: "Let's only take what we really need."

As if my thought process goes something like this: "We PROBABLY won't need this, but we have SO much extra room in the car, I think I'll just take it anyway." You never know what's going to happen when you travel with kids, but you can rest assured if you don't take it with you, you're gonna need it.

You would think, seeing as how my kids are strapped in their seats with a five-point harness, that it might be a vacation of sorts. No hitting, no pooping in the sink, no rifling through Mommy's makeup. Sadly, that is not the case. One particular road trip to Alabama to visit our families stands out in the O'Bryant Road Trip Hall of Shame.

We were scheduled to leave on a Thursday afternoon, and Zeb was to get off of work early and pick up our rental van. I did have sense enough to know that my three children were not capable of sitting next to each other in the backseat of a Toyota Highlander for nine hours without someone's blood being shed. Zeb was supposed to get off work at 3:00 P.M., and we were going to load up and head to Alabama. This would have us getting to Birmingham somewhere around midnight. But Zeb didn't get off work until 5:00 P.M., so when he went to pick up our van, they had given it to someone else.

According to the manager, who really wished he wasn't on the phone with me, "Our company does not reserve cars." He had no logical explanation for the e-mail in my in-box that read, "E-mail confirmation for your rental car reservation." Someone finally showed up at our house with a van at 6:30 P.M., three and a half hours after our planned departure.

"I hope that fool has somebody coming to pick him up, because I'm about to load this van and honk and wave when I back out of the driveway," I told my husband as we buckled all three kids into car seats.

We ended up leaving at 7:00. By 10:00 that same evening, three full hours after we left, we were approximately fifty miles from our house. We had stopped three times, and Zeb was running a fever. If you aren't great at math, that averages out to about sixteen miles per hour. I had bought a bottle warmer for the car that got lost while we were packing, so we were now stopping for the fourth time to heat up a bottle for Sadie.

As soon as we pulled into the parking lot of the gas station, Aubrey yelled, "I GOTTA PEE!"

Zeb took the bottle inside to warm it and walked Aubrey to the bathroom. I plucked Sadie from her car seat and started to nurse her. As soon as Zeb and Aubrey were out of sight and Sadie was latched on, Emma announced, "Mommy, I gots to potty. I gots to potty WEALLY bad!"

"Emma, just go in your Pull-Ups, baby," I told her. "No, I NOT BABY. I big gull, Momma. I not pee-pee Pull-Up. I pee-pee potty!"

I refrained from banging my head against the dashboard, but just barely. This same child will pull her panties down and pee on the floor beside the toilet at home, and she can't pee in Pull-Ups just this once?

"Honey, you're just going to have to hold it until Daddy gets back."

Zeb walked back to the car, handed me the bottle, and tried to get in.

"WAIT! Emma has to go."

He took a deep breath, glared at me with glassy, feverish eyes, unbuckled Emma, and headed back inside.

I was quite happy to keep my seat in the car as Zeb escorted the girls back and forth to the restroom. Because taking a toddler to a gas station bathroom is the fifth circle of hell. It doesn't matter how many times you try to explain proper bathroom etiquette to a preschooler. They are physically incapable of keeping their hands to themselves, and while you're busy having a panic attack they are working as hard as they can to discover a new disease to keep the scientists at the CDC busy for the next ten years.

It usually goes something like this: "DON'T TOUCH THAT! SQUAT, BABY, SQUAT ... NOOOOO, DON'T SIT ON IT! Aubrey, QUIT touching the little trash can!!! That's for grown-ups! I know it's just your size, but it's not for you! Nooo! Stop, stop, stop! Emma, get off the floor. Don't flush with your hand, use your foot! STOP!!!!"

Then you get to do the public restroom squat and try not to pee all over yourself while you continue to try to keep the kids out of the "little trash can." In the meantime, your thighs are shaking and burning because you haven't been to the gym since your second kid was born, and this is the best workout you are going to get for months. Finally, you get to wash one kid's hands while trying to keep the other one from touching even more disgusting stuff. It's a vicious cycle.

After sitting in the car for the better part of thirty minutes, I had a brain wave—maybe my first one of the day. When we loaded the car, we had put Aubrey and Emma in the "way back" and Sadie in the middle bucket seat. But Aubrey and Emma kept dropping stuff, so I would have to climb in the back, over all our bags and toys and coolers, and hand them things. And of course about the time I would sit down, they needed something else.

Sadie had been fine up to this point, but I realized that for anyone (meaning me) to feed her, I would have to either kneel beside her seat or lean across the entire van. This was not ap-pealing to me at all, seeing as how I had developed tendonitis in my right arm from carrying Sadie and nursing while cooking dinner, bathing my kids, driving (okay, so not while I was driving, but you get the idea)—too much multitasking! I realized that the big girls needed to be in the middle seats so they would be closer to us and that Sadie should be in the "way back" so someone could sit next to her, feed her, and sleep while the other parent was driving. You cannot imagine how thrilled Zeb was when I suggested this after his third trip to the bathroom. But, trooper that he is, he took all three car seats out and rearranged them, while his teeth were chattering with fever.

I pulled out of the parking lot as Zeb climbed into the third row of seats with Sadie and popped some ibuprofen (from a box full of medicine, about which he asked as he was loading the car, "Do we really need all of this medicine? Nobody is sick."). He propped his head up on a pillow and said, "Don't stop until we get there." Yeah, no problem—only six hundred miles to go and you're not driving.

It's important to note here that I'm seriously directionally challenged. And even though Zeb bought me a GPS for Christmas, I still get lost on a regular basis. As a matter of fact, when the little GPS voice says, "recalculating," Aubrey will say, "Awww, man, are we lost again, Momma?"

Where were we? Oh, yes. Back to the road trip (see, I told you I was challenged . . .). As I was driving along, following directions from the voice in the magic little box, suddenly the GPS directed me off the interstate through a very rural area of South Carolina. We were in the middle of nowhere, driving a route we have never driven before. It's always been all interstate, all the way. I felt like Michael Scott driving his rental car into a lake because the little voice in the GPS told him to. I was worried this wasn't actually a shortcut, but I didn't want to wake anybody up. I figured eventually I would get there, and Zeb wouldn't have to know I was lost with a GPS.

Aubrey was the only one awake, and she was totally stressing out because she could hear me talking to the GPS. I was stopped at a stop sign. It was a three-way stop and I had two choices: Turn right. Turn left. But the automated voice said, "Take a left in twenty feet." I was at a stop sign. I couldn't drive twenty feet unless I was going to drive straight through the barbed-wire fence in front of me. I had to turn first, and I had no idea which way to go. I needed to know what to do right now.

"ZEB!" I hissed toward the backseat. "The thingy is telling me to turn in twenty feet . . . what do I do?"

"Do what it says. Take a left in twenty feet."

"Yeah, but like, what do I do right now?"

"Robin, I just woke up five seconds ago. How am I supposed to know?"

Aubrey chimed in. "Awww, man! Are we lost, Momma?"

"NO, we are not! I am following the map! Sort of."

I finally guessed and ended up back on track. The magic little voice said, "Continue eight miles on North Road, then take a right."

"Momma, is 'shoot' a bad word?" Aubrey asked.

"No," I said.

Aubrey continued, "SHOOT! We're on North Road, and we don't know how to get to Shuggie's house!"

"I'M FOLLOWING THE MAP!"

"Mommy, I'm going to sleep now," Aubrey said.

"But who will Mommy talk to if you go to sleep?" I asked.

"Maybe you should talk to God."

Ya think?

After that, our trip was pretty uneventful. I stopped for gas once and drove all the way to Birmingham. We really did have a fabulous time seeing our families. It was worth every inconvenience of getting there to hold my sister's son for the first time.

But the drive home made me wonder why you don't see more mothers hitchhiking on the side of the road, because I seriously considered it. During this family visit, Zeb also had to tend to some business. And as it turned out, his meeting wrapped up early on the day before we were supposed to leave. Even though driving through the evening had been a disaster on the way to Alabama (after our fifty stops and packing and unpacking at the gas station), we still decided to head back to South Carolina that afternoon. This would give us the following day to unpack and recover from the drive before Zeb had to be back at work. I had taken the girls to a children's museum that morning, so they were worn out and asleep when we got back to my mother's house to pack everything up. I was moving at the speed of freaking light, trying to throw everything into a suitcase before my kids woke up in the car.

As I mentioned earlier, the power nap has the ability to take a perfectly good day and crap all over it. You go to all this trouble to pack extra clothes, snacks, juice, bottles, lunch, strollers, and toys to take your kids somewhere for the sole and specific purpose of making them tired enough to take a nap. Then you buckle them in their seats and speed like Bo and Luke Duke running from the law to get home before they fall asleep. If one of my kids takes so much as a ten-minute nap in the car, nap time is over. O-V-E-R. Do you understand me? Over. They are no longer exhausted, but I am. Only now I don't get to rest myself or do anything I was planning on doing while they were asleep. Plus, I get the added bonus of dealing with a child who got just enough sleep to have the energy to act like a total crackhead.

I was frantically packing, but to no avail. The kids woke up as we were backing out of the driveway. Just in time to catch one last glimpse of their grandmother and start wailing. Aubrey cried for two hours, "I want to go back to the farm"—Zeb's parents' house—"I hate Carolina, Momma. I miss my cousins; I miss my cows and my horses. I miss my chickens . . ." And on and on she went.

Emma cried for her cousin "Ella Grapes" and Shuggie and waffles. The waffles I could understand. Zeb's dad, Pop Pete, makes the best freakin' waffles you've ever tasted, and they are shaped like fun farm animals. I was starting to get a little weepy just thinking about them.

At least we started the drive back with all of the car seats in the correct position. We stopped to grab dinner and kept on driving. Things were going pretty well through most of Georgia, until Sadie woke up ready to eat. Sometime over the weekend, this child developed a deep and thorough hatred of bottles. I was primarily breastfeeding, but she was used to having one or two expressed bottles a day. But, conveniently, when I needed her to take a bottle the most, she began acting like I was trying to poison her by gagging on the nipple, or she would play dumb and act like she didn't know how to suck. She would just stare at me, motionless, while milk dribbled down her chin.

Sadie started wailing and crying real tears.

"Her wants booby milk, Momma. GIVE HER BOOBY MILK!" Aubrey and Emma began screaming at me.

"Zeb, can you pull over somewhere so I can nurse her?" I asked with an exhausted sigh.

He grabbed the GPS and found the nearest Starbucks—which I highly suspect is the real reason he bought it in the first place.

Sadie continued to scream, and I just couldn't take it. I could not sit right beside her with what she needed and just watch her cry. I took my seat belt off and pulled up my shirt and started to breastfeed her in her car seat, whilst we were driving down the interstate. I must make a disclaimer here for all you moms or moms-to-be out there who think, "Well, isn't that clever? Nursing while the baby is in the car seat! I'll have to try that."

This is not a task that just anyone can accomplish. No freakin' way. All you A and B cup ladies out there: you can go ahead and hang those hopes up. C and D cups: sorry, chicks, you'll never be able to fulfill this dream. This is a job for the Big Berthas. It took every bit of core strength, flexibility, balance, and maternal instinct that I have to keep my boob in her mouth, especially on the exit ramp.

Once we got into traffic, I put the Big Berthas away. I do have some sense of decency. We made it to Starbucks, and Zeb ran in for coffee while I took Sadie out of her seat to finish feeding her. He came back with two coffees and one hot chocolate. No offense, men, but only a man would expect two preschoolers to share hot chocolate. He handed it to Aubrey, and Emma immediately said, "I want hot shock-o-late too-ooo, Daddy."

I rolled my eyes as he went back inside to grab another cup. We were only about four hours from home now; the end was in sight. We got everyone strapped back in, blankies in place, hot chocolate in hand, DVD players in their locked and upright positions.

Zeb pulled into traffic as Sadie began throwing up. Fabulous.

"Pull over!! Sadie is puking!"

He pulled into a gas station, and I got her out of her seat and cleaned as much as I could with baby wipes. After getting her soothed and somewhat happy again, we buckled up and got back on the road.

Everything was fine, for about an hour, about the time we ended up back in rural South Carolina. Apparently, Emma gets carsick. This would have been truly valuable information to have before we gave her sixteen ounces of hot high-fructose corn syrup and started driving on winding back roads. She threw up everywhere, in her car seat, all over her clothes, in her DVD player, on her suitcase . . . everywhere.

Zeb pulled over on the side of the road; there were only cow pastures as far as the eye could see. He jerked her out of her car seat and let her finish puking on the side of the road. Then he hollered at me to hand him a towel. Now was probably not the best time to remind him that a towel wasn't on my list of "things we really needed," so I didn't.

"Ask me for anything else, but I don't have a towel."

He ripped his T-shirt off in a supersexy Daddy's Gone Wild move and started cleaning Emma up. Her clothes were covered in vomit, so we took them off. Her car seat was at least an inch deep in it. Zeb took the cover off of her seat and wadded it into a bag, but there was no way she could get back in her car seat.

At this point, my dearly beloved was standing on the side of the road, shirtless, Emma was wearing nothing but Pull-Ups and a frown, and I had whipped the Big Berthas out once again to feed Sadie. I could feel a great redneck joke brewing, but he doesn't normally enjoy my humor in times of crisis, so I kept my mouth shut. Zeb put Emma's coat on her (the only thing she hadn't thrown up on) and buckled her into a seat belt.

Now we were approximately two hours from home. Zeb was still shirtless; Emma was wearing only her jacket with the hood on, in a seat belt and crying for me to hold her hand, while

Aubrey started crying, "MOMMA, I hate Emma's frow up! Emma's frow up stinks! Momma, I HATE it!"

Sadie was latched onto one of the Big Berthas in the way back, and I had once again contorted my body so that I could breastfeed in the backseat while holding Emma's hand in the middle. (By the by, this was great for my tendonitis, and probably exactly what my doctor had in mind when he told me to rest my arm.) I was praying fervently we wouldn't get pulled over, because I had a strong feeling that Zeb and I would be going to jail and the kids were going to end up in foster care.

Aubrey started gagging, and her eyes began to water—you know what I'm talking about. "Momma (gag) I (gag) fink (gag) I (gag) gonna be (gag) sick!"

"No, you are not! Don't you dare throw up!! You want some gum or some candy?" Zeb rolled down all the windows while I started singing kid songs and digging through my purse with my one unoccupied hand to try to distract the only kid in the car who had yet to vomit. I gave Aubrey gum one piece at a time until it lost its flavor; then she would get a new one. I have never been so glad to pull into my driveway in my entire life. And I decided, like I do every time we go anywhere, that I would never, ever leave my house again.

12

. . . .

Fire the Ho

I was awake at 5:00 A.M. breastfeeding Sadie, still groggy with sleep and wondering if I could possibly breastfeed and make a pot of coffee at the same time, when Aubrey walked into the den fresh out of bed and yelled, "Fire the ho!!!"

"What?"

"FIRE THE HO!" she screamed again, this time sounding a whole lot like Yosemite Sam and bringing to mind the classic Looney Tunes cartoons we had rented only a few days before.

"OH! Fire in the hole, you mean?"

"NO, FIRE THE HO!" she said adamantly and for the third time.

I just shrugged and hoped she wasn't talking about me.

Since that day I have had many opportunities to wish she had been talking about me, to wish with all my heart that she would look at me and say in her best little Donald Trump voice, "You're firahed!" Oh, the inconveniences I could have been saved from, the hours of sleep I could have gotten, the judgmental glances I would have missed when shopping at Wal-Mart with all three kids. Even if my child had called me a whore, it would have been worth it to skip out on certain humiliating episodes.

One particular Wal-Mart trip stands out. I was pregnant with Sadie and waddling through the store with Emma and Aubrey, then two and four. I normally try to minimize the number of children I take with me to run errands, but on this day we were out of everything crucial we needed at home and both girls were out of preschool.

I was talking to one of my best friends, Amy, on my Blue-tooth earpiece as I pulled into a parking space.

"We're at the store. Let me call you back later," I said as I climbed out of the car and stuck the earpiece in the front pocket of my sweatshirt. I began unloading my kids and attempting to convince Emma that riding in the front of the shopping cart really was cool. She wasn't buying it and straightened her legs and bowed her back as I tried to force her into the seat.

"I WANNA WALK!" she screamed.

"Do you promise to stay with me and not touch anything?"

"I pwo-mise, Mommy. I not touch nuffin'."

Of course, as soon as we walked through the big double doors, both girls decided they needed to use the bathroom. Aubrey was in the "I want to pee in every potty in this town" stage, and Emma would not be outdone. Although I highly suspected nei-ther of them really had to pee, I couldn't risk it, and we made our way to the bathroom . . . where they both touched every square inch of the bathroom stall, the floor, and the feminine-hygiene mini–trash can. (Would it kill someone to put these things up a bit higher so my kids can't reach them?) I had heart palpitations as I repeated the Mommy's Public Restroom Mantra, "Stop touching that! STOP touching that! STOP TOUCHING THAT!" After scrubbing their hands as though they were prepping for surgery, we finally made our way out of the bathroom and into the store to shop.

They did really well. Emma lagged behind a little, and I occasionally had to remind her to keep her hands to herself, but we slowly made our way through the pharmacy to housewares and the entire grocery section, from the frozen foods to produce.

"Ah, sweet, sweet success!" I thought as I checked the last item off my list. We had completed our mission, and the girls were starting to get a little testy and ready to leave. My phone began to ring in the diaper bag, so I reached for my earpiece in my pocket to answer the phone. But it wasn't there. It wasn't anywhere. My phone continued to ring, as I was unable to answer it without the earpiece.

"Mommy, your phone is ringing," Aubrey told me.

"I know. I can hear it."

It was my momma, calling for our daily morning chat, and I knew she wouldn't stop calling until she reached me. I dug in my diaper bag and realized the earpiece was officially missing. I turned our caravan around and began retracing my steps through all 100,000 square feet of mega-shopping hell, scanning the floor as my phone continued to ring. I would press END, and a few minutes later Momma would call again.

It was a vicious cycle:

RING, RING, RING!

Aubrey: "Mommy, your phone is ringing."

Me: "I KNOW." (As I pressed END and hung up on my poor, unsuspecting momma).

I traced my steps all the way back to the bathroom, when

both kids decided they needed to pee again. After a quick twenty-minute potty break, I decided the best course of action would be to check out since I was at the front of the store, go by customer service, and see if anyone had turned in a Bluetooth earpiece—if not, at least I could put my groceries in my car and see if I had dropped it while I was getting out of the car.

This would have been a great plan . . . if I had any method of payment. As I loaded all my groceries onto the turnstile, I realized I had hidden my wallet under the front seat of my car earlier in the day. I didn't want to leave it in the girls' diaper bag when I dropped them off in the nursery at the gym, and it was still there—with my debit card, credit cards, and checkbook tucked inside.

"Um, ma'am . . . I, uh, I left my wallet in the car. Can I leave all of this here and run to get my money and come right back? Please . . . ," I begged, feeling my face begin to flush.

"Sure, no problem," the Nicest Cashier on the Planet replied.

The girls were playing at my feet and frantically grabbing at all the crap stores put within their reach at the checkout lines. I snatched them both up and threw them in the back of my empty buggy and hauled butt to my car with both kids screaming in unison, "I WANNA WALK!"

As we were making our way across the parking lot, I looked down and saw Aubrey had a brand new package of gum in her thieving little hands. Fab-a-lous—now my daughter was a criminal, and I was her accidental accomplice.

"AUBREY! Where did you get that?"

"Wellll, from the store . . ."

"Did you pay for it?" And if you did, why didn't you speak up and tell Mommy you had money, huh?

"Ummm, I don't think so."

"Yeah, I don't think so, either. You're taking it back, do you hear me? If you open that, you are going to be in DEEEP trouble, young lady!"

About this time we got to my car, and I unlocked the door and grabbed my wallet. As I was leaning in the door, I saw a hand-written note tucked under my windshield wiper.

"I found a pink Bluetooth earpiece right outside your car door. If it is yours, please call 555-3435."

I grabbed my cell phone and searched furiously to turn off the Bluetooth function so I could call these people. My hands were shaking with nervous energy at this point because my groceries were still sitting on the turnstile and I needed to go pay before the cashier decided I wasn't coming back. I dialed the number and the phone began ringing.

"Hello?"

"Um, hi. I think you found my earpiece . . ."

"Oh! Yes, honey, we did. We are just pulling out of the parking lot; we'll turn around and bring it to you. You just stay put!" the sweet older woman told me.

I'm not sure which parking lot this woman was talking about because a full five minutes later she pulled up in her Caddy with my earpiece.

"Thanks!" I said with a smile as I silently memorized her license plate just in case I needed to find her to harass her later . . . like, if my groceries had been put up and I had to march through Wal-Mart for a third time with my kids. I was about to come unglued.

I rushed back into the store so fast I made the little greeter-man dizzy, and I think a little pissed off because I didn't let him put a sticker on Aubrey's pack of gum. But I didn't have time for trivial details. I was racing to the finish line to get back to my groceries before they were reshelved and I had a complete and total nervous breakdown smack in the middle of Wally World.

We screeched to a stop at the checkout counter, and I sucked down some extra oxygen.

"Sorry . . . (gasp) about that (gasp) . . . I (rasping cough) . . . excuse me . . . I had to get my phone from some woman in a Caddy. Oh, and my kid stole this gum," I panted.

The cashier looked at me with pity in her eyes and said, "Don't worry about it." (Bless her . . . wherever she is, Lord . . . bless her.) This would have been the ideal time for Aubrey to turn to me, fling her hand in my face, and say, "You're firahed!" I would have gladly walked away, no questions asked. But, nooooooo, she wants to claim me when she had just committed her first petty theft.

"MOOOMMMY!" she wailed as I made her put the gum back on the shelf and apologize to the cashier. "MOMMY, hold me!! I'm sorry, Mommy! I'm SO sorry!"

Another day that nearly sent me to the motherhood unemployment line came when my two oldest were close to five and three years old. It had been a hectic month with my husband working an average of eighty to ninety hours a week. I was writing this book, waiting to hear back from superimportant New York City literary agents, and so amped up I wasn't sleeping well at night . . . or at all.

I spent the morning running errands while a babysitter watched my children so I could be home in time to feed everyone lunch and get them settled down for naps. During nap time, Aubrey and Emma slept soundly. I finished up some household chores and decided to lie down and read since everyone was quiet. I made the mistake of Tweeting my decision out into the universe. Of course, Sadie intuitively knew that I had some free time on my hands and immediately began crying from her crib.

I picked her up, and shortly afterward the big girls woke up. We went next door to visit with our neighbors, as I thought adult conversation and perhaps a beer might save me from my near-exhausted state. But upon returning home to cook dinner, I realized the swarm of flies in my kitchen window, which my husband had successfully slaughtered the day before, had sent reinforcements to seek retribution. I don't mean a few stray flies were in my house. I'm talking Sally Struthers Feed the Children swarms of flies.

I immediately called Zeb because, whilst I can handle a single bug at a time, I am ill equipped to handle swarms, hordes, or flocks of anything. While I was on the phone talking to my husband's voice mail and attempting to cook a healthy and nutritious dinner for my cherubs, they were busy grabbing flies and smushing them by the handfuls. I hope you realize I am not a germophobe—I let them eat sand—but come on! This crossed a line. Something had to be done.

I snatched open our childproof kitchen cabinet and looked for anything in a spray bottle . . . no Raid, no bug killer of any kind. Dammit. I grabbed a bottle of air freshener and took my stand at the window, in very much the same way Scarlett O'Hara faced those Yanks, I'm sure. I sprayed furiously while I held my breath and watched as a measly four flies met their Maker. This was pathetic. Scarlett would be so ashamed.

I wasn't about to load up all three of my kids at dinnertime to go to the store for Raid, but these bugs had to die. What to do? What to do?

I called my husband's cell phone again and got his voice

mail, again. (Grrrrr! Did he not realize I was in the middle of a crisis?)

It turns out that Zeb was in a meeting and unable to discuss my exterminating needs. So I did what any girl would do: I called my next-door neighbor Buck (because my daddy lives too far away). He sprayed some toxic substance that had every insect in my house flying kamikaze death spirals in two minutes flat. RIP, suckahs.

Once my husband came home, he knew I had been traumatized by the swarm of bugs and his lack of availability in the midst of my misfortune. Immediately, he asked what he could do to help.

"PLEASE, feed Sadie some rice cereal and fruit while I finish cooking."

Bless his heart. (Read: "Bless his darlin' heart and stupid head.") He poured dry rice cereal into a bowl and grabbed a bowl of applesauce. He dipped his spoon into the applesauce then stuck it in the dry cereal.

"What are you doing?" I asked him.

"Feeding her rice cereal and fruit . . ."

Was he serious? This is our third child . . . has he always fed them cereal with fruit like it was Fun Dip?

"Zeb, would you eat oatmeal like that? You have to . . . mix it . . . with form-u-la . . . ," I said, speaking very slowly.

"Oh," he said, "I just didn't want to waste any if she didn't like it."

Seriously? Seriously. Where is my pink slip?

13

· · · · · · ·

"Holy Chit" and Other Faux Cuss Words You Don't Want Your Children to Say

I'll admit it—I love to cuss. Love it. Always have. As I've gotten somewhat older but not noticeably wiser, I have struggled with my propensity toward profanity. I'm a Southern girl, wife, and mother of three—with the mouth of a sailor. I realize it's not always socially acceptable and doesn't exactly glorify the Lord the way my momma taught me. But I love it just the same. I know a lot of people say that "cursing" just shows people how ignorant you really are, because anyone with a bit of intelligence or education is articulate enough to express their feelings without using a curse word. Hogwash, I say. Sometimes a four-letter word expresses exactly how I feel and also saves me the tiring experience of trying to use a whole bunch of words when really all I need is just one. It's what we journalists like to refer to as "an economy of words."

Once I had a baby, it just didn't feel right letting those four-letter words fly like they used to. It was as if I had developed a conscience . . . a tiny one that drooled and wore a diaper. I tried in vain to be one of those mothers who say "SUGAR!" when they drop a fifteen-pound diaper bag on their bare foot. It just didn't work for me. My sweet, wonderful, and Christian mother-in-law has a talent that I envy and have tried without success to replicate: the woman can have a cussing fit without ever saying a "real" curse word. I've tried it, but I lack the creativity and chutzpah she has. I began what I like to refer to as "faux cussin'."

"Holy chit!" I'd scream when I burned myself cooking.

"Dad blast it all to heck!" I'd yelp when I hit my head on a kitchen cabinet.

"Stop FREAKIN' touching that!" I'd yell to anyone who deserved it, usually after numerous requests in a reasonable tone of voice to "STOP TOUCHING THAT RIGHT NOW!"

Freakin' was a personal favorite, until I heard it come out of my child's mouth. Sigh. I explained to Aubrey that "freakin'" wasn't exactly a bad word, but it wasn't nice either.

"But Momma," she said, her large blue eyes wide with innocence, "you say it all the time."

Aubrey and I made the first of many pacts. I would help her try not to say "freakin'" and she would help me. It was a lot harder than it sounds. We were leaving Sonic after a quick lunch one afternoon when Aubrey said, "Man, that corn dog was so freakin' good." I knew exactly how she felt, and she was right. It was freakin' amazing. I didn't want to correct her, but I also didn't want her telling her Sunday School teacher that she thought Jesus was freakin' awesome or something else slightly sacrilegious. So I reminded her of our pact and that freakin' was not a nice word.

"I'm sorry, Momma. I won't say it again," she promised.

We both did pretty well for a while, only having to remind each other occasionally. One rainy day, while my husband was at work and my two preschoolers were out of school, they begged me to bake a cake with them. I love to cook, and they love to mix and stir and make a mess, so I agreed, knowing full well what I was up against. They were going to fight over who got to stir first, who got to add which ingredients, who got to lick the beater, and who got stuck with the spoon. It would take all the self-control they possessed to keep their grimy little hands out of the cake batter until it was ready to be put in the oven and all the restraint I could muster to keep from slipping back to my favorite vice.

We cracked eggs, measured oil, sifted flour, and just made a grand old mess. My kitchen looked like the Pillsbury Doughboy had vomited all over it. I repeatedly told them to keep their hands out of the bowl, that they would be able to lick some batter when we finished mixing everything up. I'm not one of those moms who flips out because her kids want to eat a little raw cookie dough or cake batter. Lord knows I've eaten my share (and probably your share, too), and I've never had even a hint of salmonella. I washed their hands before we got started, but when you are baking with preschoolers (especially mine) there is a lot of nose picking and wedgie digging going on. This cake wasn't going anywhere but my own table, but for the love of everything that is good and holy, I did not want to eat anything that those nasty little hands had touched.

Thus began a lengthy monologue that went something like this: "Emma, stop picking your nose. Wipe your nose on the tissue. THE TISSUE. Emma, not your sister's shirt! Aubrey, stop touching her. Stop pushing! Aubrey, get your hand out of your panties. Do not put your hand in the bowl! Did you hear me? HELLO, can you hear me? STOP! GET YOUR HAND OUT OF THE BOWL. STOP IT! Use the hand sanitizer. DON'T PUT THE HAND SANITIZER IN THE BOWL! Put it on your hands, Emma! For the love!!" I finally broke under the pressure and screamed, "DON'T PUT YOUR HANDS IN THE FREAKIN' BOWL!"

"Ooooh, Momma! That's not nice," Aubrey chided me. "Don't say freakin', Momma. Just say, 'DON'T PUT YOUR HANDS IN THE BOWL!'" she shrieked to demonstrate the proper way to scream at your children. I wasn't sure if I wanted to laugh or choke them. I was not in the mood to be reprimanded by a four-year-old, but what could I say?

My husband often points out my faux cuss words and asks me if I want to hear my kids say these words. Honestly? It's better than what I really want to say. But I want to raise my kiddos right, so I've made an effort to clean up my mouth and say "sugar" when everyone in this house knows I want to say something else. My husband is definitely the calm, collected, and unflappable one out of the two of us. Of course, he's also the one who leaves the house for ten to twelve hours a day to work ... with grownups ... endless pots of coffee ... and lunch breaks ... AND gets paid in dollars for it all.

I barely have time to wipe after I pee, much less have quiet "mommy time." My only escape is leaning over the kitchen sink that serves as my prayer closet and releasing my most sincere, heartfelt prayer as I take a break from daily dish duty. "Jesus, HELP me!" I scream when I've reached my breaking point and can't take one more second of home-life high jinks.

Apparently, this behavior is rubbing off on my children. The entire family was in the car one day, and Emma could not leave her older sister alone. She pestered, aggravated, and assaulted Aubrey until Aubrey had had her fill.

"JESUS, HELP ME!" Aubrey screamed, sounding a whole lot like somebody I might know.

My husband raised his eyebrows at me and said, "How'd you like hearing your kid say that?"

"It's fine with me. I'm not taking His name in vain when I say that. I'm BEGGING for divine intervention."

Because of his blatant disapproval of my language, I was ever so surprised when Aubrey shared with me a word she learned from her daddy. Zeb had to work one Saturday, but because he is the most awesome husband alive (or possibly because he feared for his safety and the safety of his children), he stayed home until 8:30 A.M. so I could sleep late. (Yes, people without children: 8:30 A.M. is late.)

I got up, fixed my coffee, checked my e-mail, and updated my Facebook status . . . you know, all of the really important things you do first thing in the morning. Aubrey came over and asked me if I would make her pancakes. I told her I would be glad to as soon as I finished up on the computer.

She said, "But Momma, there's only one effin' egg . . ."

I still wasn't really awake. (I prefer not to speak or be spoken to until noonish, but at the time, my three kids were all under the age of four, so I rarely got my way.) I wasn't sure I heard her correctly.

"WHAT did you say?" I asked her.

"THERE is only ONE EFFIN' EGG!" She was definitely screaming at me now.

This could not be. Where would she have heard such language?

"Aubrey, what did you say?"

She shook both of her fists in the air and screamed at the top of her lungs, "DADDY WAS GOING TO MAKE PAN-CAKES THIS MORNING, BUT THERE WAS ONLY ONE EFFIN' EGG!"

Nice. I called Zeb and asked, "Was there only one effin' egg?" He paused. "There was only one effin' egg." Lovely.

I can already tell my middle child is a woman after my own heart. Her favorite phrase is "poo-poo head." It's the worst phrase she knows, and she's not afraid to use it. (Responsible party—you know who you are.) Whenever Emma feels she's not getting the attention she so justly deserves, she will scream at the top of her lungs, "POO-POO HEAD!" She's even managed to work it into her favorite songs: instead of bringing home a baby bumblebee, Emma's bringing home a baby poo-poo head, and it wasn't the itsy-bitsy spider that the rain washed out but, you guessed it, another "poo-poo head."

It's a real showstopper with the neighborhood kids and al-ways leads to a chorus of whiny, nagging voices singing in uni-son, "Emma said poo-poo head!" (In that infamous tattle-tale tone of voice . . . you know the one.) We have tried time-out, sending her to her room, ignoring her, and ostracizing her when she talks "ugly," all to no avail.

Finally, at lunchtime one day, Emma said "poo-poo head" one too many times. She wasn't even calling anybody a name; she just said it for the shock factor. In a fit of desperation, I swept her off her seat and onto the kitchen counter and did something I'd only heard about before . . . I grabbed a bottle of Crystal hot sauce. Aubrey elbowed her best friend, Tristan, at the table and said, "Ooooh, this ISN'T going to be cute!" I dabbed some hot sauce on my finger, pried Emma's mouth open, and put it on her tongue. Emma's crying was short-lived, but she was traumatized enough to tell me about a hundred times, "I not say poo-poo head anymore, Momma!" (I'm thinking, if she's repentant, it doesn't count. Right?)

Aubrey finally managed to stop saying "freakin'" just in time to learn a new and better word.

Once Aubrey started kindergarten, she was obsessed with learning how to read. Every afternoon, she came home from school knowing more sight words and sounding out even more words. She had "homework" on occasion that required her to read short little books and, to be honest, a lot of it was memorization. She was learning but not necessarily reading yet.

Shuggie was in town for a visit, and one afternoon she and Aubrey decided to read *Green Eggs and Ham*. Aubrey immediately began recognizing words on the pages.

"Shuggie! That says, 'I . . . AM . . . Sam!'" Aubrey shrieked with excitement.

She was so surprised and excited to be really reading for the first time. Shuggie coached her through several pages and helped her sound out words.

Aubrey flipped to the next page, and even though the page was covered with text, she forged ahead, sounding out words and barely stumbling over larger words like "somewhere" and "anywhere." Shuggie watched in amazement as Aubrey read an entire page all by herself.

"I do not like . . . them . . . here or . . . there . . . I do not like . . . th-em . . . Sam, I . . . am."

Aubrey looked up at Shuggie in awe and said, "Damn. I can read."

The bottom line is this: if you don't want to hear your toddler say it, you'd best keep your lip and your attitude to yourself.

Because you can just rest assured the one time you let a real stinker slip out, your child is going to hear it and save it for a special occasion (probably vacation Bible school or a PTA meeting), and all the parents are going to know she heard it from you when she uses the "f-bomb" in context and with the right inflection.

14

. . . .

Mothers of Boys:
Get Off Your High Horses

I realize I'm about to step on a lot of toes, but I don't have a problem with that. Boy Mommas, please stop acting like life is so much harder for you than it is for us Girl Mommas. I have to say that not all Boy Mommas have the condescending attitude I'm talking about, but it is far from rare. I cannot count the number of times I've run into a Boy Momma around town and, upon seeing my three blond-haired, blue-eyed "angels," she exclaims, "OH, you are so lucky you have all girls! I have all boys, and they are always dirty and making a mess and getting into trouble!"

Sigh.

I wish my life was nothing but princess dresses, Easy-Bake Ovens, makeup, and Barbies (maybe not the skanky Barbies, but anything is better than those Bratz hoes), but that is simply not the case. Apparently, when corporate was sending out memos about proper little girl behavior, they forgot to cc my kids. My girls are as rough and as mean as any boy I've ever met in my life. Yes, they enjoy a good mani/pedi as well, but just because I have girls doesn't mean it's all quiet play at my house.

I have a friend who shall remain nameless (because I would like for her to remain my friend) who has one little boy. She is forever complaining about how her little devil is always getting into everything. She likes to commiserate with me about our mischievous children, as I have one in particular that makes Dennis the Menace look like an altar boy. I was totally understanding and empathetic to all her woes—until I went to her house. Nothing in her house was childproof. Nothing. She had a three-year-old boy in her home, and there wasn't a childproof cabinet, drawer, door, or outlet cover in sight. I am totally, 100 percent serious. I was actually too dumbfounded to address her obvious oversight.

My children get into everything, and I don't have a drawer or cabinet in my house that isn't childproof. Emma already has a bright future with Cirque du Soleil or as a cat burglar. The child is uncanny in her ability to seek, destroy, and then cover her tracks. It took me two weeks to realize I wasn't having hot flashes—she was turning the heat on, in the middle of the summer, by pulling a chair up to the thermostat and then replacing it so I never suspected a thing. My husband and I gave each other the cold shoulder for the entire two weeks because we each assumed the other was messing with the thermostat.

Then there was the time I was sitting on the couch reading library books with Aubrey and Emma and saw black clouds of smoke billowing out of my kitchen. I ran to the kitchen and found my toaster oven had been turned on to 500 degrees. There were no signs of breaking and entering, just the burnt-out toaster oven as evidence of Emma's first felony: arson in the first degree.

I thought Aubrey was a mischievous toddler for continually getting into my Tupperware drawer or occasionally unrolling the toilet paper in the bathroom. Turns out that is just typical toddler behavior, and I had no idea what was coming when my second child was born.

I should have realized Emma was going to be a troublemaker when she had to be put in a cage before she was even eighteen months old. (All right, it was a crib tent, but it served the same purpose.)

We discovered her catlike agility one night after giving her an albuterol breathing treatment, also known as "baby meth." If your child ever has to take albuterol, be prepared for them to take you on a thirty-six-hour bender. She could get back out of the bed and land on her feet before I could even get out of her room—and she did, for two hours—at which point I cried, put my husband in charge, and promptly went to bed.

Emma considers herself to be quite the chef and loves to "help" me by refilling her own cereal bowl when I have the audacity to take a full four minutes in the morning to make myself a little less offensive for the general public by putting on concealer. I have cleaned enough Cheerios out of my kitchen floor to feed Brangelina's kids for a year. Aubrey was so proud of Emma's handiwork.

"Mommy, her did it ALL by herself."

"You don't say," I thought as I crunched my way across the kitchen floor. I think I'm going to start buying Cheerios and then put them directly in the trash can. That's where they all end up anyway.

Emma has exquisite taste in makeup and jewelry. Anytime she is able to bypass the childproof doorknob, pick the three dead bolts, and cut through the chain and padlock to my bedroom door, she heads straight for my vanity. The child knows the difference between a diamond and a cubic zirconium and will totally skip over the Wal-Mart makeup and go straight for the good stuff, which she promptly uses to scrawl a picture on the bathroom floor.

She also has a fetish for body art and has a secret stash of Sharpies somewhere in my house. She has adorned herself more than once with belts and bras à la Sharpie. I have no earthly idea who her supplier is. I don't remember buying Sharpies in my entire life, and I have confiscated ten of them from her in a three-week period.

Potty training with this child would have been enough for me to stop reproducing, had I not already been pregnant. Several months after Sadie was born, Emma found me in the laundry room and said, "MOM-MA ... I poo-poo in Baby Sadie ploor ..." Sure enough, there were two little nuggets waiting for me—complete with a trail of toilet paper from the bathroom all the way to Sadie's room.

But that's not even her worst. Only a few days later, I was cleaning the kitchen, and Emma came running in and screamed, "MOM-MA, I poo-poo in the sink."

I felt the blood drain from my face as I tried to comprehend what she had just told me. Excuse me, she did what?

"What did you say, Emma?"

"I poo-poo in the sink, Momma."

No, no, no, no, no. She didn't. She wouldn't. I mean, why in the world would she take her pants off in the freaking bathroom and not go in the potty? She had to be making this up.

"MOMMA, EMMA WENT POO-POO IN THE SINK!" Aubrey screamed in disgust.

I went to the bathroom to find poop in the sink, where we

wash our hands and brush our teeth. It was completely and totally disgusting, but I have to admit that I also considered it
progress. At least she was in the bathroom this time.

Emma was immediately disciplined and sent to time-out.
While I was scrubbing every surface of the bathroom with
bleach, holding back tears and trying to figure out what I could
possibly have done to deserve this, Emma was singing the blues
from time-out.

"I'ne sowwy, Momma, I weady be nice now. I not poo-poo
in da sink anymoor. Mommy? Mommy? You heah me? I not
poo-poo in da sink anymoor. I pwomise."

I was afraid to even guess where she would go instead. And
I should have been scared, because our potty-training mishaps
were about to hit the fan.

When I was approximately forty-'leven months pregnant with
Sadie, Emma came crawling into the bed with my husband and
me in the middle of the night. Normally, I would have picked
her up and put her back in her own bed, but I was too pregnant
to pick her up, and she was being really still and quiet. So, we
snuggled. I was lying on my left side, and she nestled up against
me. I kissed her little cheeks and she said, "cwratch my armpits,
Momma," and I did. (I don't know why she likes to have her
armpits scratched, but it's her favorite thing in the entire world.)

As I was scratching I began to notice a smell. Not a poop
smell. A morning breath meets strep-throat smell. You moms
and nurses out there know what I'm talking about. I thought to
myself, "Poor baby, her throat probably hurts so bad she can't
sleep. I probably need to take her to the doctor in the morning."
I was lying there feeling sorry for her and scratching her tiny
little armpits and skinny little arms, when she opened her fist
and put something in my hand . . . something small . . . some-

thing round . . . something slightly sticky. The scream that is-sued forth from my lips could have gotten me a part in any horror movie.

"AAAAAAAGHHH! Oh my God, oh my God, OH MY GOD! ZEEEEEB!!"

Zeb sat straight up in the bed, looking for an armed intruder. "WHAT? WHAT IS IT?"

"HOLY CHIT! Emma just crapped and put it in my hand!" I screamed as I flipped on all the lights. "She crapped on me! ZEB, SHE CRAPPED ON ME!"

My child—my baby—had just crawled into my bed and handed me a turd.

A turd.

My child literally just crapped on me. My mind could hardly take it in. What in the hell did this mean? Who was I supposed to call about this? My mother? Supernanny Jo Frost? Dr. Phil? Oprah? I had never, in my whole entire life, heard of someone whose child had crapped in their freaking hand.

I was in shock, totally grossed out . . . and my bed had been violated. After a 3:00 A.M. bath for Emma, some vigorous hand washing on my part, and a quick sheet change, we all got back into bed. I avoided eye contact with Zeb for the next twenty-four hours, hoping against hope that if we didn't talk about it, maybe it hadn't really happened. It was all just a bad, bad dream.

My point is this: just because my child is in a smocked dress, with a hair bow adorning her golden Shirley Temple curls, does not mean she is as sweet or easy as she looks. I realize that there are fundamental differences in raising boys and girls. Boys like to play with trucks and guns. Girls like to play dress up and with makeup. Boys have a penis, girls have a coo-coo—or whatever you call it in your house. A child's temperament determines how easy, difficult, mischievous, or compliant they are, and, like it or not, temperament doesn't have anything to do with what sex they are. Sometimes, little girls wear hair bows simply to hide their horns. And until your little boy has crapped in your hand, I don't want to hear what a handful he is.

Wal-Mart, Porn, and the FBI

In 2006, two life-shattering events occurred: the house I grew up in was broken into and burned to the ground, taking with it every earthly possession my mother owned, and both of my maternal grandparents passed away after fighting illnesses for many years. I had just had my second child in less than two years in a town I had only lived in for three short months. Because my husband is completely incoherent in the middle of the night, I was getting up every time one of our girls woke up, banking on being able to nap every day.

It wasn't out of the ordinary for me to put a sign on the door telling folks to not ring the doorbell while we were sleeping. Sometimes the only sleep I would get in a twenty-four-hour period would be during nap time. It requires an unprecedented level of skill to get a newborn and a toddler to sleep at the same time—if I ever enter a beauty pageant, I plan on using this as my talent. Needless to say, nap time is sacred at my house, and with the levels of stress I was experiencing in my personal life, I needed all the sleep I could get.

You can only imagine my joy one fine afternoon when the doorbell started ringing just as I was drifting off. We had an odd-shaped window right beside the door, for which I could never find a curtain, so once I was spotted by two young Mormons, I could no longer pretend I wasn't home. I wrapped my bathrobe around me and walked to the door.

Now, I watch *Dateline* and *Oprah,* and I wasn't about to open the door for two well-dressed men I had never seen before. My momma didn't raise no fool. I leaned against the window and screamed at them, "We don't want any, and I'm trying to sleep! Go away!"

The young men looked confused and screamed back, "Do you know who we are?"

"I don't care. I'm trying to sleep. GO AWAY!"

"Ma'am," one of the men screamed as he flipped open his badge, "we're with the FBI."

Gulp.

I immediately had butterflies in the pit of my stomach the size of the turkey on my momma's kitchen table every Thanksgiving. This was worse than the time I had a note taken by my sixth-grade teacher with multiple curse words in my own handwriting. And worse than the numerous times I'd been called to the principal's office in high school . . . combined. What in the world could they want with me? And holy chit, I just yelled at the FBI!

I slowly opened the door. "How can I help you?"

"Ma'am, we're here because child-pornographic images have been traced back to your IP address."

Knock me over with a feather. "Huh? WHAT did you just say?"

"We have traced known pornographic images back to your computer."

"I'm sorry, but that is impossible. Could it just be pictures of my kids in the bathtub or something like that?"

"No, ma'am, that's not considered pornographic. These are known images of children being molested, and they are on your computer. Are you the only one who uses the computer?"

"No, my husband uses it, too. But I'm telling you, this is NOT possible."

To say I was in complete and total shock would be like saying Michael Jackson had a little work done. I was flabbergasted. The FBI agent reached into his pocket and pulled out a photo. It was of a young girl being molested; the obscene parts had been blacked out. But it was sick and disturbing, and if it was on my computer, I was going to beat the hell out of somebody.

The agents said that they needed to interview anyone who used the computer and that, if my husband wasn't home, they could come back at a more convenient time. I asked them to wait at the door and, with shaking hands, called my husband at work as I quickly got dressed. "You need to come home right now and talk to the two FBI agents who are here." Zeb thought I was playing a sick joke on him until I started sobbing uncontrollably.

I know my husband. At the time we had been married for ten years. We've been together since we were eighteen, and I knew there was no way he was capable of this. As hard as it is for some men to believe, my husband finds all pornography disgusting and demeaning. It has never mattered to him how fat I am or what my hair looked like; he has never so much as glanced at another woman since we've been together. For some unknown reason, I am all he wants and needs.

I let the agents in the house. (Yes, I made them stand on my front porch while I called my husband AND my daddy and threw some clothes on.) I told them my husband was on his way home, because we wanted to clear this matter up immediately. I am not good at nervous small talk, as you may recall from my appointment with my plastic surgeon about my boobalas, and I was about to soil myself trying to convince these people that my husband wasn't capable of such monstrosities.

Me: "I'm sure y'all are really good judges of character and you'll see as soon as you meet him that this isn't possible. I don't even know when he would look at it. He goes to bed early, and I'm up all hours of the night with the babies, so it's not like he could sneak in here and do it then. I'm sorry I'm chattering so much. I haven't slept in a while and we just got back from my grandfather's funeral in Alabama and I've been really upset." (Why was I talking so much? Shut up, Robin. SHUT UP! You sound more guilty with every word!)

Agent: "Did your husband go with you?"

Me: "Oh, no. Not for the whole time, he flew in for the funeral . . ."

The agents exchanged meaningful eye contact, like "AHA, that's when he did it."

CRAP! They were good at this. I was so nervous, I was ready to go all Chunk from *The Goonies* and start confessing every bad thing I'd ever done in my entire life.

Me: "He wouldn't do this, I'm telling you."

Agent: "Ma'am, with all respect, we hear that every day."

Me: "If y'all find child porn on my computer, he's going to be glad you're here, because I'm going to beat the living CHIT out of him. Do you understand me? You'll be here for his protection, because I'm going to kill him!"

About this time Zeb walked in the front door, nervous as I had ever seen him. The men all shook hands and exchanged greetings, and Zeb asked the agents what he could do to clear things up.

"We have a program that we can run on your computer to scan for the images, if they are there, it will pull them up . . ."

Zeb began to explain to the freaking FBI why he believes the Internet should be free—boyfriend can be a little communist in his political beliefs sometimes—and because of this belief, he has left our wireless access unencrypted, thus leaving our Internet connection open to every freeloading pervert in the neighborhood. Zeb continued to ask the agents how they would feel "hypothetically speaking" if they found some not-exactly-legal copies of movies on our computer.

This explained his nervousness to me, but really made me want to throttle him. I mean, could we just maybe, I dunno—cooperate with the FBI? Hel-lo? Earth to Zeb!

"Do it," I interrupted. "Run the program. If there's porn of any kind on my computer, I want to see it."

Every conspiracy-theory movie and book I'd ever digested chose this moment to give me the worst media-inspired reflux I've ever experienced. I had split-second premonitions that their software didn't look for pornography but planted it. They needed a scapegoat, a patsy. They found some liberal, free-thinking, pseudo-communist and knew it would be the perfect setup. Zeb was going to jail, and I would end up working with Oprah and the Innocence Project to prove his innocence. We would lose the house because I wouldn't be able to afford it after going back to work and paying for day care. I wondered which of our friends would let me and the kids sleep on their futons and which would shun us.

The agents ran their computer program as Zeb and I waited anxiously. They didn't find one single pornographic image on our computer. (Boo-yah! How ya feelin', FBI?) One agent looked Zeb square in the eye and said, "Sir, I'd highly recommend encrypting your wireless connection." My nerves were so frazzled after they left, I drank a big glass of Mommy Juice (refilled seven or eight times) and lay down for a nap (as I could no longer sit upright).

Several weeks went by, and I assumed that my brush with child pornography was a thing of my past. (A slightly hazy memory, thanks to Mommy Juice . . .) I ordered some online prints of my two girls from our local Wal-Mart. I went to pick them up with both of my children in tow. It was summertime, and there were lots of pictures of the girls playing at the beach, in sprinklers, and in our backyard baby pool.

My children love to be "nekkid" more than anything in the universe, so there were quite a few heinie shots. One of my personal favorites was of Aubrey, who was two at the time. She had gotten one of my mixing bowls from the kitchen, filled it with water, and was sitting in it naked as the day she was born. The bowl was so small, only her feet and her tiny little booty fit inside it.

The clerk in the photo lab gave me my prints, and I quickly leafed through them before I paid for them. I noticed that many of my pictures were missing, and in their place was a piece of paper that read, "Several of your photographs were deemed inappropriate by management. Due to their pornographic nature Wal-Mart has chosen not to print them."

I felt my face flush, and I heard brakes squealing in my head. Excuse me, but they think I'm a child pornographer, and all they have to say about it is, "You can't have your pictures?" Oh, heeeell to the no. I don't think so.

I turned to the clerk. "Excuse me, ma'am. I'm missing some of my pictures, and there must be some mistake because they were NOT pornographic. They were just of my kids running around in our backyard."

The clerk looked flustered as she replied, "Well, ma'am, I was working last night, and I asked my manager about those prints, and he said we weren't supposed to print ANY nudity . . ."

"I'm sorry. Don't you print pictures of men in bathing suits all the time? Naked babies fresh out of the womb? You can't possibly be serious."

"It's our store policy. I'm sorry for the inconvenience."

Inconvenience, my right foot!!! There was no way I was going down like this. I wasn't about to be accused of being a child pornographer (again!) without throwing a good old-fashioned hissy fit. I gave a silent prayer of thanks that my children were not yet old enough to be humiliated by me.

I looked the clerk in the eye and threw down the gauntlet. "I need to speak with your manager, NOW."

The manager came out and gave me the same spiel as the clerk, apologizing profusely but still refusing to give me my pictures. This was not working out for me, at all.

"Let me see if I understand you both correctly. You think that my pictures were pornographic in nature, and all you have to say to me is 'I'm sorry'? You think I was EXPLOITING A CHILD and YOU are apologizing to ME? Is that right?"

They looked nervously at one another but didn't say a word.

"Here's the deal, people. My kids run around in my backyard butt-nekkid ALL the time, and I want to document it. My baby book is full of pictures of me doing the exact same thing. Those pictures are in NO way pornographic . . ."

I thought back to my recent visit from the FBI but didn't bring up that I had actually seen child porn before and that these photos weren't even in the same ballpark. Somehow, I didn't think it would strengthen my case, so I decided to keep that little tidbit to myself. I continued to rant with increasing volume as Emma screamed from her car seat, which was propped in the cart, and Aubrey stood up in the back of the cart and took off her dress. She stood there naked for a few minutes while she turned it inside out and then put it back on.

"If you think I'm a child pornographer and all you have to say is I can't have my pictures, then SHAME ON YOU! You either call the police RIGHT NOW and have me arrested or GIVE ME MY FREAKIN' PICTURES!"

The manager was sweating bullets as he quietly printed the rest of my pictures, slipped them into an envelope, and passed them across the counter, without saying one word.

16

. . . .

Dinnertime Drama

Why is it, exactly, that no matter what I am eating, my children must have a bite? I have spent the better part of more days than I care to count trying to eat something, anything, that my children wouldn't want a bite of or wouldn't try to appropriate for themselves.

I find it hard to believe the pancakes on my plate taste any different than the ones on my three-year-old's plate. Truly, the only thing I have to do to get my children to try a new vegetable at this point is pretend I'm going to eat it myself and then refuse to share.

My sweet mother-in-law used to howl at my husband and his four siblings, "It wouldn't matter if I was eating a plate of dog crap, you'd STILL want a bite!" And I believe it.

Panic ensues if my children think I have something they do not, or cannot, have.

"Mommy, Mommy . . . PLEASE, I want some. I'm soooo hungry."

Hungry? After three chicken nuggets, a heaping helping of macaroni and cheese, and a pile of steamed broccoli? I think not.

"You aren't hungry," I want to scream, "you're jealous of my food! You can't stand for me to have something that is mine!"

"But I AM hun-ga-ry, Mommy. I weally am!" Emma will protest. At three years old she barely weighed twenty-five pounds, but to this day my little angel can eat more than my husband.

"What do you want?"

"Ummm, I fink I want a see-sah sah-wid," she'll say as she eyes my low-fat Caesar salad with grilled chicken. What a coincidence.

I picture myself running to my room, locking my bedroom door, and hiding under my bed to eat in peace . . . or ordering a pizza and having it delivered to my bedroom window so I don't have to touch every slice in the box to find the right match for each child.

"Thanks for calling Papa John's, can I take your order?"

"I want a medium thin-crust supreme pizza, and I'll pay extra for the delivery guy to sneak through my neighbor's yard, scale my fence, and bring it to my bedroom window. If one of my kids sees him, I'm not tipping."

Or maybe I should just start going through drive-throughs and eating while they watch helplessly from the backseat—locked into place by their five-point harnesses. But I don't do any of these things—I make another plate of food, or even another see-sah sah-wid for them.

I've heard these people who say, "I'm not a short-order cook; I'm only cooking one meal, and my kids will eat what I make or be hungry." Maybe you are simply a better mother than I am and all of your kids eat whatever you put in front of them. But I have a picky eater at my house, and unless everybody is eating french fries, Easy Mac, chicken nuggets, and Oreos for dinner, we aren't all going to be happily eating the same thing every night.

I don't fancy myself a short-order cook, either, but I would like for my children to be well fed and eat of their own volition. I have no desire to have a Supernanny Jo Frost showdown at the kitchen table every time we sit down to eat. If that means I have to make steamed broccoli every single night so they can eat a vegetable they like, so be it.

I would rather let my children try something new and say, "No, thank you, I don't care for that," than listen to them cry at the table until they finish their carrots, or what have you.

There are a lot of things you can make your children do, but making them put food in their mouths, chew, and swallow are not on that list, as evidenced by the Sunday Soup Standoff of 2008. Aubrey and my husband went head-to-head in a battle of the wills over a bowl of homemade vegetable soup. Aubrey chose to sit in time-out for hours instead of taking one bite of soup. Kids: 1. Adults: 0.

My point is further proved by the Green Bean Incident of 1989, when Linda Murphy, our next-door neighbor and surrogate mother, tried to make my sister Blair eat one green bean. Blair tried without success to convince Linda she did not like green beans. Linda would not be dissuaded and kept on until Blair finally chewed and swallowed a single green bean. But my baby sister firmly proved her point by promptly throwing up all over the kitchen table. Kids: 2. Adults: 0.

I've seen the scorecard and realize that odds are this is a battle I'm not going to win. I'll take a "No, thank you" over puking at the dinner table any day . . . but that's just me.

I am a Southern girl; I was born and raised in the great state of Alabama. My momma taught me how to make cornbread, how to pray, and how important it is to have family dinners several times a week. Nothing says "down-home goodness" like the whole family sitting around the dinner table passing the gravy and talking about the day's events. Even though I have three young daughters and life gets really hectic, I still try to have a sit-down, home-cooked meal several nights a week.

Momma taught me to cook "from scratch," but sometimes a girl's gotta do what a girl's gotta do, and every once in a while I have to take a few shortcuts. It's hard enough making gravy when you're holding your two-year-old and trying to calmly discipline your four-year-old Supernanny-style without spilling your Mommy Juice, but once you start breastfeeding your infant whilst doing all these other things (save the Mommy Juice—I do have standards, people), it's damn near impossible to keep the gravy from burning.

Because of this, I have developed a few quick and easy meals that wouldn't shame Momma too badly. One of these go-to meals consists of premarinated pork tenderloin with steamed rice and broccoli. It's quick, easy, and delicious. But most important, every member of my family will eat it (as long as there is ketchup involved). I was preparing this standard meal one evening when something went horribly, horribly wrong.

As I was removing the tenderloin from its package, part of it broke off. No big disaster—I just lined it up where it had broken off and placed it in the oven. About twenty minutes later, I opened the oven to check on it and screamed as I was sexually harassed by my dinner for the first time in my entire life. There, in my very own oven, was the largest penis I had ever seen. I was equal parts horrified, fascinated, and really, really impressed.

Naturally, I did what any good Southern girl would do . . . I grabbed my camera while screaming at my kids, "Hot! Hot! Hot! GET AWAY FROM THE OVEN! IT'S HOT!" Then I took a picture to send to my sister and closest friends. I must say it is one of the only times I have been truly offended by my dinner (the other being the time I was served "chicken knuckle soup" in Thailand). It was impossible to keep a straight face as my husband walked in from work and asked, "What's for dinner?"

When I could wipe away my tears of laughter and finally speak I replied, "I believe Juno would call it a pork sword."

Pamper Yourself

Women love to tell a new mom, "Don't forget to take care of YOU. If Momma's not happy, then nobody's happy." Before you had a child, you probably thought they meant going for a monthly massage or pedicure. You had no way of knowing they actually meant, "Close the door when you pee so you can have sixty seconds to make your grocery list" or, "Be sure and lock the door when you get in the bathtub so you don't look like you're bathing in the baby pool at the YMCA on the hottest day of summer." You couldn't know; you were pregnant and full of hopes and dreams . . . and still believed the lies sold to you by Johnson & Johnson commercials and Pampers' multimillion-dollar ad campaigns.

I used to get my toes done once a month. The more kids I have had, the less frequently I have had the money or, more important, the time to sit still while someone massages my feet and paints my toenails. I have developed a pedicure especially for moms that you can do in your own home, in your own time, in only five short days.

Day 1: Remove old crusty nail polish from eight toes, left over from the last time you had a "real" pedicure (probably about the time your last child was born or the last time you had to have your feet in stirrups). Break up a fight between the kids, cook dinner, feed the baby, and clean the kitchen. Take a shower, realize you never finished taking off your polish, remove nail polish from remaining two toes. Clip three toenails, put your four-year-old back in the bed, get water three times for your two-year-old until the ice-to-water ratio is exactly right and you finally get the cup she wanted, feed the baby. Collapse in the bed from exhaustion.

Day 2: Wake up at 4:00 A.M., feed the baby. Get back in bed for a few hours. Get up again at 6:30 A.M., get dressed, put on makeup. Finish clipping toenails and possibly filing them. Make lunches and serve breakfast, take your kids to school. Run errands, feed the baby, clean house, pick kids up, put kids down for naps, feed the baby. Apply base coat. Collapse in bed from exhaustion. Get up, cook dinner, clean kitchen, bath time, feed baby, bed time. Then—you got it—collapse in bed from exhaustion.

Day 3: Congratulations, today you get to apply your first coat of color—to six toes—until your four-year-old diva catches you and demands a mani/pedi. Do laundry, feed the baby, fold and put away clothes. Make lunch. Feed the baby. Naps. Feed the baby. Dinner. Feed the baby. Collapse in bed.

Day 4: Feed the baby, make breakfast, make lunches. Take the kids to school. Go to the grocery store, put up groceries. Come home and feed the baby, clean the bathrooms, and apply a second coat of color. Feed the baby. Pick the kids up, put them down for naps. Feed the baby. Dinner. Baths. Proceed to the bed, collapse, and sleep if anyone will let you.

Day 5: If there is any nail polish left on your toes, you may now apply your top coat. If not, you get to remove your already-chipped toenail polish and begin the whole process again.

Wasn't that fun and so relaxing? Can you believe you ever left the comfort of your own home to waste your money for someone else to do this for you, when all this time you could have been doing it yourself?

Going to the spa and the salon are not your only two options for "mommy time." After tucking my kids into bed every night, I fill my bathtub with scalding-hot water and bubble bath and grab a good book. Several nights a week my husband will take over the bath and bedtime routine, and I will slip into my bedroom early to relax for a few minutes.

When I was about thirteen months pregnant with my third child, I had slipped away for a long, hot, and quiet soak. The only sounds I heard were the muffled screams of my children as they fought tooth and nail with their poor daddy over which toothbrush was whose and which pajamas they wanted to wear. All of a sudden the bathroom door came crashing open as Emma came running into the room, shattering the silence. She began stripping at the door and was totally "nekkid" by the time she reached the tub.

"I wanna take a bath wichu, Momma!"

I sighed. "Fine, get in."

About that time, Aubrey came walking into the bathroom and yelled, "HEY! No fair! I want to get in your bathtub, too!"

"Whatever," I said. I was too exhausted to argue with them or try to scream for my husband to get his kids out of my bathtub.

They splashed and played for a few minutes before Aubrey turned to me and said, "I think you're too fat for this bathtub. You need to get out."

I knew full well I was exceeding the weight limit for that bathtub, but we don't have a zoo in Charleston, so I couldn't exactly call the hippos and tell them to scoot over and make some room for me.

"Actually," I told her as I gently kicked her out, "this is MY bathtub. I set the weight limit, and YOU, my dear, are much too small. Go find your daddy."

Date night is another important part of taking care of yourself, but you need to go ahead and prepare yourself that date night isn't going to be anything like it used to be. First off, your husband, who used to get dressed all by himself to wine and dine you, can no longer find a pair of underwear or socks without your assistance. Secondly, you have to have a babysitter. Which boils down to this: you have to have the permission of a fourteen-year-old girl to go out to dinner with your very own husband.

I used to go to dinner with my husband B.C. and talk about our future, my work, his work, life in general. Now when we go out to dinner, we usually fight through our appetizers and salads about things we haven't been able to discuss in front of our children. By the time our entrees are on the table, we are ready to play nice and move on.

One date night, as we argued our way through appetizers, Zeb made an announcement. "From now on, we are getting a babysitter on Friday nights so we can go to Taco Bell, eat bean burritos, act like rednecks, and yell at each other. Then on Saturday night, we'll go somewhere nice and actually enjoy being together."

I actually got food poisoning on that date and ended up

pulling double duty on the toilet when we got home. Taco Bell would have probably been a safer dinner choice.

You know it's been awhile since you've been out on a date with your husband when you have to go to the mall on your date in order to buy clothes to wear for your date. The standard Mommy Uniform of matching sweats and puke-stained T-shirts is usually not the best date-night ensemble.

After a trip to a local festival that had been held in the middle of muddy strawberry fields, my one and only pair of jeans were no longer suitable for anything other than cutting grass or perhaps a trip to the Flora-Bama (a honky-tonk on the Florida-Alabama state line and a mecca to Southerners). Thanks to what is known as the "in-between stage" of postpartum weight loss, I had one pair of pants to my name that didn't have an elastic waistband, and they were trashed. My mother was visiting and my husband wanted me to go out to dinner with friends.

I knew I was in trouble in the pants department but thought I might be able to find a pair that would work. I dug out an old pair of Levis, slathered some Vaseline on my butt and thighs, and pulled them on. I buttoned them, butt (heh-heh) breathing was no longer an option. My husband walked through the bathroom as I sucked my stomach in and attempted to zip my pants.

"Babe, you look cute," he said.

I rolled my eyes.

"What?"

"I can't sit down in these pants, much less sit and eat."

I explained to my husband that I only had one pair of pants to my name and that they were unsuitable for public viewing. He called our friends and told them we would be a few minutes late. Then the Best Husband in the Entire World took me shopping to get new clothes. I won't reveal the name, but I will say it's the first time I had bought clothes in over a year from a store that didn't have shopping carts or a snack bar.

I stood in the dressing room in nothing but my Spanx and nursing bra and waited for Zeb to purchase my date-night ensemble. As I waited, I was hopeful that this night would end better than the last date, when I paid a babysitter to watch my kids while I contracted food poisoning. Ah, happy endings . . . new clothes and no vomiting or diarrhea.

Having kids changes everything from your definition of a pedicure to the places you choose to shop to the way you date your husband. My advice? Take every second the little devils will let you have to yourself . . . whether that is standing in your girdle and nursing bra in the changing room at your favorite store or sitting on the potty taking care of business with the door blissfully dead-bolted.

18

. . . .

In Sickness and in Health

The thing I miss most about my life B.C. is the luxury of being sick all by myself. Gone are the days of sitting luxuriously on the toilet as the latest gastrointestinal bug rips its way through my body. No more calling in sick to lie in bed for days on end reading trashy tabloid magazines while sucking on Luden's Cherry Cough Drops and recovering from a bad sinus infection. Nope. Those days are over.

The only person who usually cares when I'm sick is my husband, and mostly because that means he has even more work to do when he comes home. When any member of my family is sick, I rush to their aid with Popsicles, medicine, or hot tea, whatever the situation requires—I am prepared. And I'm not complaining. I am a mother and a registered nurse. I am a nurturer.

I just think it would be really nice if someone in my house could bring me a roll of toilet paper when I am stranded on the toilet with diarrhea instead of standing in the bathroom, watching, and listening to Mommy's Musical Bowels, holding their nose and trying to peek in between my legs while saying, "Ewwww, it stinks in here, Mommy!"

Here's a novel idea: get out.

Thankfully for my family, the worst sickness we have ever had to deal with was a particularly nasty stomach bug Emma contracted when she was only five months old. We had lived in Savannah, Georgia, for a few short months and only had a few acquaintances. When we were told by our doctor to head to the hospital so Emma could get IV fluids, we realized we had a problem. Zeb had to work, I had to be at the hospital with Emma, and we had nothing to do with Aubrey.

I called Gena, an acquaintance I had met through a church mothers' group. And I do mean an acquaintance—not a friend. Not yet, anyway. We had met for playdates with our children on a handful of occasions and barely knew each other, but her father was a well-respected pastor in Savannah and a pillar of the community, which was one of the only reasons I did something so horrifying that I shudder now even thinking of it.

I called a woman I barely knew at the time and asked her if my two-year-old (who had never spent the night away from home) could come and stay at her house . . . indefinitely. I was aghast. Firstly, because I really didn't know her that well (but I figured at least half the folks in town knew who her daddy was if she tried to run off with my kid), and secondly because who calls a woman who has a two-year-old and five-month-old of her own and says, "Would you like an extra toddler to take care of for a few days? Oh, and a member of her immediate family has just been hospitalized with a highly contagious stomach virus . . . thanks so much! 'Kay, buh-bye!"

But Gena was more than willing to help me out and agreed to let Aubrey come and play until Zeb could come and pick her up—which would have been great, if I hadn't started vomiting about four o'clock in the afternoon the day before Emma was to be released from the hospital.

In between breastfeeding Emma, holding her so she wouldn't rip out her IV, and vomiting in the trash can, I called my husband at work and told him I needed some major help.

Emma couldn't stay in the hospital by herself, and I could no longer sit upright; I was burning up with fever and needed to go home and sleep.

Zeb headed to the hospital, and I called Gena to see if Aubrey could stay a little longer.

"I think if I go home and lay down until I feel better, then I can come and get her," I told Gena.

"Why don't you go home and take a nap and call me when you wake up, and I'll just bring her to you after dinner and baths, so you don't have to get out of the house?" Gena suggested.

As soon as Zeb got to the hospital, I began the five-minute drive home. I was as focused on the road as I could be while doubled over with stomach cramps and shivering uncontrollably with fever.

Ding-ding-ding-ding!

The gas light dinged at me. All I wanted to do was go home and finish puking until my stomach officially turned inside out, and now I had to stop to get gas.

I swung into a gas station, slammed my car in park, and decided to put in just enough gas to get the needle off of empty. I would pay inside and buy a box of Saltine crackers and some Gatorade so I wouldn't have to leave the house again.

I pumped gas until I had to throw up again and leaned over the trash can by the pump. Maybe now I could make it inside, grab my stuff, pay for everything, and get back outside the store before I need to puke again. I really, really didn't want to throw up in the store.

I ran through the store like a contestant on *Supermarket Sweep* and snatched everything I needed off the shelves. By the time I got to the checkout counter, a line had formed and, wonder of all wonders, the cashier had on a name tag that read HI! I'M TRACY AND I'M IN TRAINING! I sighed to myself as I mentally reviewed every cuss word I knew.

I stood in line pondering what I could have done to offend God so badly and inched forward, still shivering with fever, as Tracy slowly rang up every customer in the line.

Finally, it was my turn.

I threw my crackers and lemon-lime Gatorade on the counter and muttered, "Pump number six," while swallowing down the bile that was rising in the back of my throat.

"I'm sorry, couldn't hear you, dear . . . what was that?" Tracy asked with a cheerful smile.

"Pump SIX," I said through gritted teeth.

"Alrighty, let's see . . . seven dollars on pump six, a box of crackers, and a bottle of Gatorade . . . will that be all?"

Why do people ask you this when you check out? Obviously this is all I was going to buy—I was standing at the checkout line staring at her with nothing in my hand but a debit card.

I nodded my head very slowly.

"M'kay," she said as she scanned everything and asked, "Would you like a bag?"

Seriously? Could she not tell I was the same color as the Gatorade? I mean, I do realize I have a bachelor's degree in nursing, but I don't think it takes a degree in the medical field to deduce from my purchases that I was feeling less than stellar and she should maybe . . . I dunno . . . hurry the HELL up!

"Whatever," I replied, starting to let my irritation show.

"Oops," Tracy said with a shy little grin. "I accidentally rang your crackers up twice . . . let me see if I remember how to take them off . . ."

Sweet, sweet Jesus, help me. I was sweating and shaking and about sixty seconds from spewing again.

"I DON'T CARE! I'LL PAY FOR 'EM!" I yelled at her.

Tracy looked up, her smile fading as she realized she might have her first testy customer on her hands. "Well ma'am, if you'll just wait one second I'll take them off!" she huffed at me.

"Look," I said, leaning across the counter toward her bulletproof glass, "I am sick and about to puke all over this store. I need to pay. NOW!"

"Oh!" she said. "Well, grab an extra box on your way out!"

Finally, I blissfully slid my debit card through its slot and went outside to puke beside my car again.

I got home at 6:00 P.M. and figured I could sleep for at least two hours before Gena would call, ready to bring Aubrey home. I stripped out of my clothes and jumped into bed with my cell phone volume set on high. I pulled the covers over my head and fell into a deep, dreamless, and feverish sleep.

I slept through roughly fifteen missed calls (Gena, Zeb, my mother, Gena, Zeb, Gena, etc.) and woke up at 2:30 A.M. in just enough time to make one very important, split-second decision: I could (a) puke all over my brand new carpet or (b) puke all over my brand new bedding. Scrubbing vomit out of my carpet on my hands and knees did not sound like a good time, so I threw the comforter off of the bed and threw up all over my sheets.

Now, if I hadn't had children, I could have put a clean set of sheets on my bed, taken a shower, and climbed back in bed to sleep the rest of the day away, watching *Judge Judy* and *Oprah* whenever I woke up. But I had to get a shower, put clothes on, and go get my babies.

"I tried to call you last night," Zeb said as I walked into the hospital room. "Gena called, and I didn't know what to tell her. I couldn't leave, and we couldn't get you."

I apologized and explained that I had totally blacked out as soon as I got in bed. I took Emma from him, so he could stretch. As he stood up out of the recliner, I noticed that his color wasn't great and that he didn't have the same spring in his step he usually had.

"Do you feel okay?" I asked him.

"Yeah, just stiff from sleeping in this chair, and I got really hungry in the middle of the night and the only thing I could find to eat that wasn't junk food was a can of peaches in the vending machine. I think they may have been bad."

He went to bring the car around to the patient-loading zone while I gathered all of our belongings. As we were putting Emma in the car, Zeb looked at me and said quite matter-of-factly, "I'm about to throw up."

"What? Why are you telling me?"

"Because I'm not sure what to do about it . . . where am I supposed to throw up?"

I pointed to some bushes off to the side of the main entrance of the very large and very busy university hospital. I climbed in the car and started the engine to listen to some tunes while my husband threw up in the bushes.

As Zeb stumbled into the car, the man actually said out loud, "I knew I shouldn't have eaten that can of peaches. I guess they were bad."

I would like to state for the record that my husband is a genius. Literally. His ACT scores were nearly perfect, and you should never, ever play Trivial Pursuit with him unless (a) you are on his team or (b) you want to go home crying like a little girl because you feel so insignificant and stupid. But on occasion, common sense seems to elude him.

"I'm sorry. I'm not sure I understand you. Are you saying you just threw up because you ate a bad can of peaches?"

The man looked me dead in the eye and said with a straight face, "Well, what else could it be?"

"Oh, I don't know, maybe the same LETHAL stomach virus that your wife and daughter have . . . the virus that made your daughter so sick that WE ARE JUST NOW LEAVING THE HOSPITAL!"

"Nah. I'm pretty sure it was the peaches. I feel fine now."

I shut my mouth as he pulled out of the hospital parking lot to drive us home. Peaches, indeed! This brought to mind a similar incident when I had made a huge vat of vegetable soup with veggies from our very own garden, and, after eating one bowl of soup and almost an entire chocolate chocolate-chip pound cake, he told his mother my soup made him sick. Peaches, my right foot! We'd see about that when he was still puking in twelve hours.

He deposited me at home with the baby, and I unfolded our sofa bed to prepare for an intense day of watching movies on the couch with the kids. Zeb went to pick up Aubrey from Gena's house before she had a chance to call Child Protective Services and have us charged with neglect, and then he took Aubrey to preschool.

He staggered in the door about an hour later and collapsed beside me on the sofa bed, where I was weakly entertaining Emma.

"So, are you still feeling better?" I asked snidely.

"I was fine until I got to Aubrey's school. I was trying to unbuckle her car seat and realized I wasn't finished throwing up."

"What did you do?"

"I ran to the front of the car, and I puked all over the church parking lot, in front of all the parents. I'm pretty sure the grandparents in the car next to me thought I was hungover and bringing my kid to school."

"What was Aubrey doing?"

"Laughing so hard she was wheezing."

"Man," I said without taking my eyes off Emma, "I bet you're really sorry you ate those peaches."

Grandmothers, MeeMaws, and Mimis

Growing up, I only knew there was one type of grandmother and that was the kind that I had. But once my friends and I started having kids and turning our mothers into grandmothers, I realized that all grandmothers are not created equal. As far as I can tell, there are three basic types of grandmothers: Grandmothers, MeeMaws, and Mimis. You might know them by different names, but I'd be willing to bet that you can fit every grandmother you know into one of these three categories.

Grandmothers are the most formal of the three. They complain when you open the refrigerator and let the cold air out—although I'm not sure there's another way to get food out of the refrigerator without opening the door. Their formal living room is just that . . . very formal, and not only are you banned from sitting on the furniture, which may or may not be covered in plastic, but if you so much as walk across the carpet, they will know. Grandmothers wear pantyhose and pumps, get perms once a month, and always have a purse to match their shoes. They do important things like play bridge and don't ever miss Sunday school.

MeeMaws don't care much about their shoes or their hair, unless it's Sunday morning. And their uniform of choice is an old housedress with a well-used apron tied around their necks to keep grease from staining their clothes when frying okra for your dinner along with four or five other vegetables and a pot roast so tender you could eat it with a spoon. MeeMaws don't care about you letting the cold air out of the fridge. They expect you to eat when you come to their house because "You ain't nothin' but skin and bones!"

Mimis are a newer breed of grandmother. They are still working, to pay for their next round of plastic surgery, and only want to keep the grandkids overnight if it's not going to interfere with their bikini wax. Mimis get their nails done once a week and are constantly reminding their daughters and (gasp) their daughters-in-law not to "let yourself go," by saying helpful things such as, "You look so pretty when you have your hair highlighted. It makes you look less mousy" or, "You're going to look so good when you lose all that baby weight." Mimis are trendy and stylish, they never ever go gray, and most likely have a tiny, obnoxious little dog à la Paris Hilton. When their children call with the latest anecdote about what Junior has done, you can be sure Mimi will follow up with Muffy's latest adventure.

Mimis liked to be called Mimi and other such names because it sounds much less grandmotherly than MeeMaw, Nana, or the Mimi equivalent of kryptonite . . . Granny. If you want to really piss these women off, just go ahead and call them the G word. Not that you'll be able to tell they are pissed: their faces have been frozen in time by the miracle known as Botox since their eleventh twenty-ninth birthday.

I am triple blessed in that my momma, my sweet mother-in-law, and my kids' pseudo-grandmother, our next-door neighbor, Nana, all fall into the rarest of all categories, one that is quite hard to classify. But I refer to them collectively as "Shuggies" because this is what my children have dubbed my mother. These women have mastered the fine art of being grandmothers; they know exactly where the line is between being a blessing and spoiling your kids rotten. They are so loving and so much fun that if you were to give your kids the choice between going to Grandmama's house or the circus, the kids will pick Grandmama every time.

I went ahead and provided Webster's definition of a Shuggie for your convenience . . .

Shuggie: n. slang, derivative of the Latin meaning "Sugar Momma." A grandmother or older woman who gives tirelessly of her time, money, energy, and love to anyone and everyone. She expects nothing in return. She can sleep in any climate or environment, regardless of temperature and/or sleeping conditions, including but not limited to: sleeping on a pool float, a mattress in a garage, or in a double bed with two squirming and sweaty preschoolers. A Shuggie's diet may vary depending on her surroundings and how many other hungry mouths need to be fed. It is common for a Shuggie to wait for small children and young, exhausted mothers to eat before ever even considering her own hunger. A Shuggie is also known for driving great distances in order to put others' needs ahead of her own. To find a Shuggie of your very own, you'll have to pray; only God knows how to make something this good.

Being a grandmother, from what I hear from these women, is even better than being a mother. I can totally see how you get all the joys, half the heartache, and none of the discipline and how, at the end of a long day, you get to call their parents and tell them to "Come get your kids." Sounds like good times to me, unless you are one of those unfortunate grandmothers who never told your own children no and now you are raising your grandbabies.

My hat's off to some of you women, because you really couldn't help that your child went off the deep end, so to speak, and got mixed up in some bad stuff . . . drugs, alcoholism, abusive relationships, and the like. You women are just being true, selfless Shuggies and trying to save those babies from their parents. But some of you just need to grow a pair and tell your child to come get their kids and give them a copy of the Yellow Pages open to CHILDCARE CENTERS.

It just isn't right for young parents of this generation to expect their parents to be free day-care centers. It makes me furious! Our parents have worked, slaved, and saved to retire and relax, not so you can save a buck or two on day care in order to pay for you and your baby daddy to go to Panama City Beach, Florida, for spring break every year.

Grandparents ought to be the ones allowed to spoil your kids. They shouldn't have to discipline them. If you are doing it right at home, your kids will behave for Nana and Papa. If they're behaving and I'm not around, I say go ahead and give my kids a Popsicle before dinner. I'm not going to let them do it at my house, but they should be able to have fun and break some rules with the grandparents.

Unless you're a Mimi, there comes a point in every woman's life when you might need to start asking for fashion advice from someone younger than you (and by younger I mean someone who cannot yet qualify for the AARP). Momma asked my sister and me years ago to please let her know if she started dressing like an old woman, and we solemnly swore that we would.

There's something to be said for evolving with fashion. Just because you had a great wardrobe in the 80s or 90s does not mean you should be wearing those clothes now. Even though they were cute, when you hang on to old trends you end up looking . . . well, old.

My sister and I have only had to call Momma out a few times. Once, when she had on pantyhose with open-toed shoes and (GASP) no toenail polish! We let her know as gently as possible that if you can see the seams in the toes of your pantyhose, you ought not be wearing them and that if you can see your toes, they should look like you've been to a salon in the last decade.

My momma's got style. The woman knows how to accessorize like Coco Chanel and is one of the rare women in this day and age who has boldly gone gray and refused to color her hair. She's got a head of salt-and-pepper hair that would make George Clooney cry. She deserves a standing ovation for that, I think. My own grandfather went to his grave thinking his wife had never had a gray hair on her head . . . Lord, have mercy.

The only other fashion faux pas I almost had to address with my momma was the passing of her dear old friend . . . the fanny pack. See, my husband had a work trip in Orlando, and I decided this would be a fine time to take our girls to Disney World, even though I had a three-month-old who was still breastfeeding. His company was going to pay for part of the trip, so we decided to go. Shuggie offered to either stay home with the baby or go with us. It was easier to take the baby and breastfeed than to walk around Disney with a breast pump and expressed milk, so we decided everyone would go. Thus began the Quest for a Fanny Pack.

She came to South Carolina the week before we left to help me pack and spend some time with the girls. Every time we walked into a store to buy supplies for the trip, she would ask me, "Now, where do you think the fanny packs would be?"

I wanted to say, "Probably on aisle 1987 . . ."

But I didn't . . . because she's my momma. If she wanted a fanny pack, well, I figured the least I could do was help her find one. And besides, Hulk Hogan has one to match every outfit and surely he doesn't have those things custom made. I was sure we would find one somewhere.

To my great surprise and Shuggie's great disappointment, we never found one. I could see her eyes glaze over with Fanny Pack Envy every time we passed someone with one strapped around their waist in the Magic Kingdom. I swore to myself if I found one with mouse ears that made her butt look like Mickey Mouse, I would buy one for her, no matter the cost. After scouring the gift shops, I came to the conclusion that Hulk Hogan does indeed have his fanny packs custom made, because if the Mouse doesn't sell them, then who does?

Another thing I've noticed recently is the gradual role reversal between my mother and me. Gone is the woman who would go from zero to redneck in five seconds flat if she thought you might scratch her hardwood floors. Shuggie claps along while my children tap dance on my hardwood floors.

Where is the Coaster Nazi of my youth? On her last visit to my house, my mother attempted to spray my sofa down with Febreze and clean some of the stained upholstery. I haven't bothered, because, really, what is the point when I still have one child who is only halfway potty trained and one who isn't even eating solid foods yet?

But I digress. Shuggie spent a good hour cleaning spots off

of my sofa, which I appreciated since I never would have attempted it myself. Then she went to bed and left a glass of ice water sweating on the arm of the couch she had just cleaned. She left it there all night long, and when we woke up the next morning, there was a water spot covering three-fourths of the arm of the sofa. I swear it's just like having a teenager.

While we were in Disney World, my kids' very favorite thing to do was going down the water slide at the hotel's swimming pool. Shuggie hopped in the pool with them while I relaxed in the shade reading Celia Rivenbark, wiping my tears of laughter, and fanning my baby's sweet little face with the battery-operated fan I had purchased for such occasions.

Shuggie kept getting alarmingly close to the bottom of the slide. She was just trying to get a good view of the top of the slide to see when her babies were coming down so she could catch them. But, Lord have mercy, the lifeguard shouted himself hoarse trying to tell her to back away from the slide. Granted, he was yelling, "YOUNG LADY! YOUNG LADY! STEP AWAY FROM THE SLIDE!" Which I'm sure would have confused even me. I mean, let's just face it—even I haven't been called "young lady" in quite some time.

You are probably thinking, "Why didn't he just get up and tell her she was too close to the slide?" That, my friend, is a wonderful question, and the answer is quite simple—because he easily weighed 350 pounds. Getting up would have required him to get out of his perch in the lifeguard's chair, which I'm pretty sure involved an intricate system of levers and pulleys that would have shamed the Egyptians.

I was so entertained by my mother's oblivious rebellion and the lifeguard's obvious annoyance that I had to put my book down so I could focus on the situation as it unfolded in front of me. I noticed several other vacationers doing the same thing.

As my children climbed the back of the slide, Shuggie would inch closer and closer to the slide until she was touching it. The lifeguard would subsequently start yelling, "YOUNG LADY!" until the girls came swooshing down the slide in their green froggy life jackets and safely into their grandmother's arms. The only break in this cycle was the time it took them to climb the stairs and wait for their turn in line.

My mother had no idea he was talking to her, and he faced the daunting task of getting out of his chair if he was going to continue to look like the all-powerful Barney Fife of a lifeguard he truly was.

Shuggie finally pushed him too far when she began allowing my two preschoolers to climb on the obviously decorative rocks that formed an island in the center of the pool. I unfortunately missed the harness and crane required to get him out of the chair as I was discreetly trying to breastfeed my baby and pay attention to the unfolding drama. I looked up as my baby latched on, just in time to see the man waddling around the edge of the pool, making his way to my momma.

Now you "big-boned" folks, don't get your panties in a wad. I am a nurse, and I used to try to guess folks' weight as they came in to the triage office in the ER, just to keep my mind busy. I would guess in kilograms and pounds, then see how close I was when they stepped on the scales. I was never off more than a few ounces. So when I say he weighed 350 pounds . . . he weighed 350 pounds. (It's also comforting to know that I have a second career in the carnival industry if this whole writer thing doesn't work out.)

If you want to be morbidly obese on your own time, that is just fine with me. However, if your job requires you to be able to rescue someone drowning in a swimming pool, I think (a) you should be able to walk with your feet less than three feet apart and not have thighs so big you can't get them closer together, (b) you should look vaguely like David Hasselhoff in his *Baywatch* days, and (c) you should actually be able to swim; floating, in my humble opinion, is self-serving, and while it may save your life, it doesn't help me one little bit.

He finally made his way over to my momma and told her to get the kids off the rocks and, while she was at it, to quit touching the freakin' slide. (I'm paraphrasing here; I was still sitting on my butt in the shade being thoroughly entertained by this whole fiasco, so I couldn't exactly hear what they were saying.) He had his hands where his hips should've been, and she was looking at him like, "You are NOT the boss of me . . . WHAT-EV-ER!" Shuggie was totally clueless he had been yelling at her for the better part of an hour. He, of course, had no idea she hadn't heard a single word he had said.

I explained the situation to her on our way back to the room, and she said, "Why didn't you tell me?"

"Are you kidding me? That's the most fun I've had at Disney World in my entire life."

20

· · · · · · ·

Good Game

I've spent my entire motherhood trying to convince my children how special they are. Not in an "I'm more important than other kids, center of the universe, everything revolves around me" kind of way, but in a more subtle "God made you special and exactly the way He wanted to" kind of way.

As a child, I was covered with freckles and I hated them. I don't know why. Just a typical woman thing, I guess—always wanting what I didn't have. My oldest daughter, Aubrey, has the same smattering of freckles across her nose and cheeks that I had, and they are precious. I tell her often how much I love her "sprinkles" and that I'm so glad God decided to give them to her.

I never complain (in front of my daughters, anyway) about how my body looks or how clothes fit or don't fit. And if they ever catch me standing on the bathroom scale and ask, "What's that say, Momma?" I always reply, "Just right!"

The media and starving Hollywood starlets will have their influence soon enough, and I intend to instill as much confidence and stability in them as I possibly can before that happens. I want them to have healthy body images and scoff at the toothpicks the media tries to put on display as "ideal."

When my children ask, "Why are we going to the gym AGAIN, Mommy?" I always tell them it's because I want to be healthy and strong, which is true, although losing a few more pounds is usually on the agenda as well.

I took Aubrey and Emma for a summertime swim with my friend Courtney and her two boys. At the time, Sadie was roughly six months old, and unlike Gwyneth Paltrow, Madonna, and the rest of those skanks with a six-pack and a six-month-old, I actually looked like I'd had a baby. I was still trying to lose my baby weight. And I knew I would. I'd done it twice before; it just takes me some time, and I have to work hard for every single pound. (I'm talking Spinning classes, weight training, and a diet that would make Bob Greene cry for something fried or chocolate.)

At any rate, we were at the pool and Aubrey was filled with a sudden gush of love and enthusiasm for me. She wrapped her arms around me, hugged me, and said, "Do you have a really big belly, Mommy?"

My sweet friend Courtney was like, "Nooooo, Aubrey! She doesn't!" (She is sweet, but she is also a little bit of a liar.)

I took the opportunity to remind Aubrey that, just a few short months ago, there was a person living in there and that it might take a little more time before I looked like I used to.

Aubrey looked at me with concern in her eyes and asked, "Will it ever be little again, Mommy?"

Good question. Let's hope so.

"Yes, baby. That is why Mommy goes to the gym to exercise, to be healthy and help my tummy get smaller."

A few days later, we went to Target to let the girls spend

some of the birthday money their grandparents had sent to them. We made an entire morning out of going to the store and deciding on the one perfect toy they both wanted.

In a turn of events very shocking to any mother of daughters, they both decided they had to have another Mermaid Skank . . . er, Mermaid Barbie, to be exact. They were happy as pigs in mud with their purchases and spent a good portion of the day in our indoor swimming pool (the bathtub, people).

As I was cooking dinner, Aubrey came running into the kitchen with her little purple-finned skank, pointed at the doll's abnormally small waistline, and asked, "Mommy, your belly gonna get that little?"

I heaved a big sigh as I replied, "Sure, baby."

"Well, it's going to take a LOOONG, LOOOONG, LOOOOOOONG time! Huh, Mommy?"

"Go get back in the tub, Aubrey."

My efforts in the area of my children's self-esteem have not been limited to their body images, though. I continued to try and assure them that they are valuable simply being who God made them to be and being kind to others.

One particular conversation I had with Aubrey left me wondering if I had been going about this all wrong. I was breastfeeding Sadie when she was only a few months old, and Aubrey was leaning over my lap to look at her and snuggle close to her face.

Aubrey looked at me with love in her eyes. "Momma, I love her so much. You love me so much, too. Right, Momma?"

"Of course I do."

"You love me the most. Right, Momma? Cause God made me so special. Huh, Momma?" she continued.

"Aubrey, I love you all the most. You are ALL so special to me and to God."

"Uh-uh!" Aubrey screamed, outraged. "God made ME special! And nobody else!"

Wait a minute. What? This is not what I had been working toward for the past five years.

"Aubrey, God made us all equal. He loves everybody in the world the same. He thinks we are all special." I struggled to come up with terms Aubrey could process in her young mind. "You don't love one of your sisters more than the other one, do you?"

Aubrey folded her arms across her chest and began tapping her foot and scowling at me. She puckered her lips up in a full pout and pointed at Sadie.

"What? Why are you pointing at her?" I asked.

"I love Sadie the best. She is my best sister in the whole world. Her doesn't pull my hair or bite me OR snatch my toys like Emma does!"

For the love.

"No, she doesn't. But does she swim, dance, and play ska—um, I mean, Barbies—or Play-Doh with you?"

"No," she answered abruptly.

"Does she sing with you, go to school with you, or play hide-and-seek with you?"

"Noooooo," Aubrey said, this time not as adamantly.

"Who does all those things with you?"

She sighed in disgust. "Emma."

"I guess that makes Emma a pretty special sister, too. Huh?"

"I guess so," Aubrey said as she rolled her four-year-old eyes and walked away.

And while Aubrey often delights in Emma's punishments, Emma cannot imagine a fate worse than seeing her big sister get into trouble.

On another afternoon spent playing outside, the big girls

were having a blast making "soup" full of sticks, rocks, and dirt in a large pot they had borrowed from my kitchen. It was all fun and games until Aubrey decided to pick up the ginormous glass and stainless-steel lid and bash Emma's head with it like she was crashing cymbals together. The attack was totally unprovoked; I had witnessed the entire thing as I sat on a bench feeding Sadie her bottle.

Aubrey was immediately exiled to time-out. I set the kitchen timer for five minutes and told her I didn't want to hear one word out of her until the timer went off, or we would start over. After approximately forty-five seconds, Emma came into the den crying and said, "Momma, can my sister come pway wif me? Her is sooo sobby."

"Honey, she is in time-out for hitting you."

There was still complete silence radiating from the time-out corner.

Emma began crying, "But Momma, I wub her, and I want to pway wif her . . ."

I sighed as I hefted her into my lap and wondered when Emma would finally have enough of her sister's brutalities that she would welcome Aubrey's time-out as a cease-fire of sorts. A time to take refuge, to run around the house and touch all of Aubrey's favorite toys while her older sister watched helplessly from the corner—that day wasn't as far away as I thought it might be.

The very next morning, I walked in on a heated argument over a Barbie doll (stupid little skanks—they are nothing but trouble in this house). I came in just in time to see Aubrey shove Emma. She looked up and saw me and said, "Oops! I'm sorry, Momma. I'm sorry. I didn't mean it! It was just an accident . . . I, uh, I was just giving her a 'Good Game.'"

We have a family tradition going back to my childhood of giving family members a "Good Game." You know how athletes are always patting each other on the butt and saying, "Good Game"? Except at our house it's not about the act the person is actually performing but more about the element of surprise. Emma loves to give me a "Good Game" as I unload the dishwasher, fill the bathtub up with water, or bend over to pull clothes out of the dryer. The "Good Game" must come out of the blue and be totally random to actually be funny. And it's always funny.

I didn't say a word to Aubrey but simply pointed to the time-out corner. Shoving someone definitely did not qualify as a "Good Game."

Aubrey quietly assumed the position as I set the kitchen timer. Emma marched into the kitchen, and I sighed as I mentally prepared myself for another round of consoling the victim as her tormentor sat unimpressed in the naughty spot.

Emma walked right past me and up to her sister, stomped on her toes, and flexed her tiny little arms à la Hulk Hogan, right in Aubrey's face, in a very "You want some of THIS?!" move.

Aubrey held her toes and cried. It was all I could do to keep from slapping Emma on her tiny heinie and giving her a "Good Game" for finally standing up to her big sister. I tried to wipe the smile off my face as I assigned Emma her own corner.

21
. . . .

Froggy Faith

When Aubrey was four, she caught the tiniest frog I've ever seen right outside our front door. I put the penny-sized frog in a Mason jar and poked holes in the lid and wondered if we could keep him alive for twenty-four hours. Aubrey's class just happened to be learning about the letter *F*, and the following day was show-and-tell. If we could keep this frog alive, Aubrey would be the most popular kid in her class and I could finally secure my Mother of the Year nomination.

I wanted to help her become the It Girl in her preschool class but was wary of my ability to sustain his little life for an entire twenty-four hours.

"Aubrey, we are going to have to let him go in a little while because he will die without food."

"But MOMMA! I will feed him!"

"Honey, I don't even know what he eats . . ."

She sighed, exasperated at my ignorance. "He eats BUGS, Momma! And his name is Fred."

Obviously frogs eat bugs, but where was I supposed to find bugs small enough to feed "Fred"? The average housefly was half his size.

As the day went on, Aubrey pushed Fred and his Mason jar in her baby-doll stroller, spun him around in our office chair, and I even found her hiding under the sheets in her bed with the jar unscrewed "tickling his belly." We have never had pets, and Aubrey was overjoyed to have something to be in charge of.

She was running and jumping and being her normal, wild four-year-old self with him. After a particularly precarious jump from her bed to Emma's bed with Fred's jar clutched under her arm, I thought he was a goner. He was still, very still—maybe too still. I told her, "Aubrey, you have to be SO careful with the frog. He is just a tiny little guy, and you REALLY scared him!"

I got distracted playing with Emma and looked up a few seconds later when I heard Aubrey having church with Fred. She was peering into the jar and quoting 2 Timothy 1:7 to her frog, "God hasssth not given you a ssthpirit of fear but power, love and a sssthound mind! God is with you, do not be afraid!!" We repeat this verse at night when she's scared.

"Momma, he's moving!"

Thank you, Jesus. Can I get an "Amen"?

The next morning, we woke up to find Fred lying flat on his back with his arms and legs stretched out. He was belly-up in the Mason jar, and we had a serious problem.

"Shhh, he is sleeping!" Aubrey hissed at me.

Fred had, in fact, entered into his eternal slumber.

Obviously, I couldn't let her take a dead frog to school (unless Mrs. Emily was interested in having Fred's Froggy Funeral, which I highly doubted).

"Aubrey, Fred is . . . um, well, he's not sleeping. Fred is dead. He is in froggy heaven with Jesus."

"OH, NO!" She gasped, slapping her hands to her cheeks.

I started making suggestions of other things she could take for show-and-tell that also began with the letter *F*. But she could not be dissuaded.

"Mommy, I REALLY wanted to take my tiny little frog!"

"If you hurry up and get dressed, we can look outside for another one. But listen up, girly, we probably aren't going to find another one. You'd better start praying NOW that God helps you find one," I told her as I finished pulling her curls back from her face and fastening her hair bow.

Aubrey immediately clasped her hands together and prayed. "God, will you PLEASE help me find a new frog?" She paused for a split second before yelling, "Thank you! He said YES, Momma!"

Once everyone was dressed and ready for school, we marched outside to look for a frog the size of a fingernail. Aubrey, Emma, and I searched the front yard to no avail, while I continued to make suggestions of other things she could take for show-and-tell.

"But, but, but Momma, I REALLY want to take my tiny frog!"

I sighed, and we soldiered on to the backyard. By this time I was getting a little antsy; we only had five minutes before we needed to be in the car on our way to school. Aubrey and Emma kept calling, "HEEEERE FROGGY, FROGGY, FROGGY!"

When, suddenly, I looked down and saw a frog that made Fred look morbidly obese. I screamed, "There's one, Aubrey, get it!" (She does the catching. I don't touch frogs.) She grabbed him in her tiny little fist and shouted, "YESSS! Thank you, JESUS!" Emma pumped her fist in the air and whooped, "ALL-WHIGHT! Woo-hoo!" They were giddy with excitement.

We deposited Fred Junior into the recently vacated Mason jar and raced to the car. I quickly buckled Aubrey and Emma into their car seats, and as I was backing out of the driveway, I saw Aubrey with her face pressed against the jar, whispering, "I'm sthorry about your friend!"

As we walked into school, Aubrey proudly displayed her frog to everyone she passed and made sure to tell every harried mother and still-groggy child, "God gave me anudder frog!"

Her preschool class was awed by Fred Junior's sheer cuteness, and Mrs. Emily, God bless her, turned recess into an opportunity to release Junior back into the wild, lest he meet the same fate as his namesake. May he rest in peace.

22

. . . .

School Daze

When Aubrey started kindergarten, I didn't sob uncontrollably and insist on carrying her into her classroom on my hip. I didn't have to struggle to keep my emotions in check. It was quite the opposite, in fact; Aubrey had been so defiant and rebellious for the weeks leading up to school that I was relieved to have a few hours of peace and quiet.

Maybe I should've felt guilty about not being upset, but I didn't. I had done my job as her mother and her teacher for the last five years, and while I enjoyed every second (well, some of them, anyway), it was time for someone else to take a turn. Don't get me wrong; I love my children more than anything on the face of the earth. But I was looking forward to the next chapter of our lives. Kids grow up for a reason: if they stayed any one age for too long, it would kill their parents.

I had spent the three weeks before school started in Time-Out Boot Camp, trying desperately to maintain a consistent disciplinary approach with Aubrey, who had become increasingly more strong-willed and smart-mouthed. Not to mention that during the same time, my children had passed around a stomach virus, a head cold, and a sinus infection. I was exhausted.

Aubrey woke up bright-eyed and excited about going to school for the first time. The whole family walked Aubrey to school that morning for her special day. I helped her find her seat, her cubby, and the water fountain and gave her a quick kiss before I left. We stopped in the doorway to take a few more pictures, and as we turned to leave the classroom, I saw Emma standing in the doorway blowing kiss after kiss to her big sister and best friend.

And fine—I was a teeny bit sad. I cried a little.

But it wasn't a selfish sad. It wasn't because I thought I was losing my baby, felt like I was useless, or even felt older now that Aubrey was in school. I was sad for Aubrey and Emma as sisters and best friends.

Their entire lives they had known nothing but each other. It never mattered how often we had to move for my husband's work. We didn't have to worry about making friends; they were inseparable and together, no matter where we were.

I knew I was going to miss her. I knew I was going to miss my wake-up calls, when she would crawl into my bed before dawn and whisper in my ear, "Hold me like a sthpoon, Momma" before she curled up next to me and fell back asleep. No more sleeping late. I would actually have to set an alarm and get up before someone cried or climbed into my bed.

Our Pajama Days, or days when my three girls and I would stay in our pajamas all day long while I cooked, cleaned, and organized, were over. The long days of Aubrey and Emma playing together in their pajamas or, more often than not, just their princess panties were over.

Although Emma and Sadie were still home for the time being, cooking wasn't the same with Aubrey in school. I missed both of my helpers dragging dining chairs up to the kitchen island so they could stand tall and fight over whose turn it was to stir. I missed having Aubrey grab a pile of clean, folded laundry so she could refold it (read: wad up into a wrinkled mess) and "help" me.

But mostly I missed listening to her play with Emma. I missed their constant chatter and make-believe play. I missed watching them change into every princess dress they have in less than thirty minutes and overhearing Aubrey direct their imaginary princess lives. I missed watching Aubrey tie a rope around Emma's waist, then tether her sister to her tricycle as they reenacted scenes from *101 Dalmatians.*

I missed their giggles and constant conversation when they were supposed to be napping, and oh, my God, I missed nap time! No more shutting out the world from 1:00 P.M. to 4:00 P.M. every day. Nope, my two youngest and I sat in the carpool line at 2:30 every single day.

Aubrey normally thinks she can do everything by herself, from brushing her teeth to crossing the street, but when it's time to get dressed for school, she is as helpless as a newborn babe. During her first year of school, if I could have left Sadie and Emma at home asleep while I got Aubrey dressed, packed, and dropped off to school, then I would've had time to put Aubrey's socks on and fasten the Velcro on her shoes for her when she claimed, "I don't know how, Momma. I really don't."

But since I didn't want to have Social Services take my kids, I couldn't leave them in their beds sleeping while I took their sister to school. So Aubrey learned that she was going to have to buck up and do some things herself that she would rather let me do for her.

One morning, while I packed Aubrey's lunch, changed a diaper, and fed her younger sisters, she managed to put her socks on her own two feet. But, apparently, the shoes were just too much. So when I walked out to my car to take my first load of kids and stuff to the car, Aubrey followed me. In her socks, in the rain . . . with five minutes to get her to school.

I buckled Sadie into her car seat and left Emma with instructions to "BUCKLE UP RIGHT NOW!" and ran back inside to find a clean and dry pair of socks. Preferably two that matched. I helped Aubrey change her socks and put her shoes on her feet. We ran back out to the car to find Emma sitting in the passenger side of my car, with all the doors locked—shoving DVDs into the DVD player, one after another after another.

"Good morning!" a cheery neighbor called out.

"Um, hi . . ." Distracted, I waved, right before I began beating on my car window and bellowing at Emma. "Emma O'Bryant, if you know what's good for you, you'd better unlock those doors RIGHT NOW!"

Getting ready for school was a chore, and now we'd have to do it every day . . . for the next eighteen years. I heard all you mommas of older children saying, "Enjoy being home with your babies; it goes by so fast." I did not realize you were saying this because it gets harder! I thought you just meant that they are babies for such a short amount of time that I should enjoy the time I have with them. I really had no idea that the toddler years were the "easy" part.

Consider this my public service announcement to all of you hardworking moms of toddlers out there—it gets easier, but it gets harder.

Eventually, you won't have the option of staying in pajamas

all day long; you will have to get dressed and go somewhere. And whether you are a morning person or not, you will have to get up, feed and dress your kids, and get out of your house before eight o'clock in the morning.

The transition was hard for me . . . I had no idea kindergarten would be this hard. Aubrey seemed to be doing fine, until she came home from school one afternoon totally exhausted and fell apart. She began sobbing and telling me how much she hated school.

"Momma, I meeeeed you! Rock me like a baby, Momma." I held her and rocked her like the baby she still was and did my best to console her.

"Kindergarten is so hard! I hate it!" She stopped talking briefly to gasp for air.

"I know it's hard, honey. I'm sorry."

She sniffled and lifted her head off my chest. "Mommy, after kindergarten . . . will I be done with school forever?"

"Well, not exactly," I said. I didn't have the heart to tell her how many years she had left.

"But why, Momma? WHY??? I hate it so much! I do. I hate kindergarten. It is so freakin' hard!" She was crying so hard that snot was running down her nose and her face was red. I didn't dare correct her usage of "freakin'."

"Because, honey, you have to learn how to read and write. Do you want to be as big as Mommy and still have to have me read stories to you?"

"NOOOOO! But Momma, it is so HARD! I hab to do my work . . . and then, and then, I hab to go to recess . . ." Her voice cracked as she broke down at the stressful memories of four whole days of recess. "And then, Momma, I have to do my work, and eat in the cap-a-teria, and THEN I HAVE TO TAKE A NAP! AND HAVE A SNACK! I HATE IT, MOMMA. I HATE IT!" She was inconsolable.

"Honey, don't you want to learn to read and write like Mommy and Daddy? Then when you grow up, you can have a good job that you like."

Just to try to take her mind away from her painful kindergarten nap-time memories, I asked, "What do you want to do when you get big? Daddy builds things, and Mommy writes newspaper articles and books. What would you like to do?"

She picked her head up off my chest and took a shaky breath before looking me dead in the eye and saying, "I fink . . . I fink I want to write Facebooks, Momma."

Well, chit. How was I supposed to explain to her that, even though Facebook can technically be considered a full-time job, Farmville won't pay the bills or put actual food on the table?

23

· · · · · · ·

Eff the PTA and Their Effin' Carpool Line

I was beyond excited when Aubrey started kindergarten. I thought I would have so much extra time during the day to write, work out, and get things done around the house. Life was going to get easier. Not only was my child going to be in school learning and blossoming for roughly eight hours a day, but I wasn't even going to have to get out of my car to get her there.

Lots of schools have carpool lines these days. It is a simple concept. You wait in a line, single file. Just like you learned when you were in school. When you pull up in front of the actual school building, you let your child out of the car and scratch off to Starbucks or for your weekly pedicure . . . or to go home to clean the toilets, whatever.

But, alas, someone somewhere will screw up even the simplest of concepts for everyone involved.

The tricky part, it seems, is not the dropping off of the child but the picking up. At Aubrey's South Carolina elementary school, different grade levels get dismissed at different times, to keep traffic flowing. The kindergartners are released at 2:30, the first and second graders get out five minutes later, and so on, with the fifth graders getting out of school at 2:45.

Now, I'm no rocket scientist, but I do know how to tell time (if the clock is digital), and it seems to me that if I know my child isn't going to be let out of the building until almost 3:00, I might not want to be the first one in the carpool line at, say, 2:25. But, apparently, there is more than one adult in Mount Pleasant, South Carolina, who doesn't understand that they are backing up traffic for miles because they decided to get in the carpool line twenty minutes before their child gets out of school. And because I am stuck in line behind them, blocked in by cones on one side and a sidewalk full of students on the other, I conveniently get to wait with them until their child gets out of school.

After getting stuck in the carpool line twice in two days, I decided to try another tactic. I got to the school five minutes early, like I always do, and backed into a parking place that allowed me to see directly across the parking lot to the side of the school. This was a brilliant idea, I thought to myself. Emma and Sadie were happy in the backseat. Emma was watching a movie on the DVD player, and Sadie was happily gumming her toes and cooing to Emma in the car seat beside her. I could sit there with my babies until I saw Aubrey's class coming out of the building, jump out of the car, run across the parking lot, and be back in my car before the Super Mommy next to me had time to speed-dial Child Protective Services.

"MOM-MY! I dwop my sippy cup!" Emma yelled from the backseat.

I twisted around in my seat to reach her cup, and as I righted myself, I pounded the steering wheel in disgust.

"AAAAAGGHHH! You can NOT be serious!" I screamed

at the gold minivan that had just driven directly in front of me to park on a grassy knoll that was most definitely not a parking space.

"What is wrong with these people? You give a woman a minivan, and all of a sudden she thinks she can just make up her own parking spaces! Just because you have your whole life written in bumper stickers on the back of your car DOESN'T give you the right to park wherever you want to! I don't care how many honor students and goldfish you have!"

I opened my car door and stood in the door frame to see over her ridiculously wide van and looked for Aubrey's class. I caught the minivan driver looking at me right before I spotted Aubrey, and I did my very best to stare her into shame as I clumsily climbed down off my car. I continued muttering as I walked past her open window. "I really can't believe the nerve of some people! I got here early with TWO KIDS, TWO, and parked in a REAL LIVE parking space, and she thinks she can just wheel in here at the last minute and park wherever she wants!" I was furious, but I was smart enough to snatch Aubrey and run before a member of the PTA called Child Protective Services on me for walking ten feet away from my car with my two children still in it.

As ridiculous as these people are, they'd do it. I know they would.

The members of the PTA were brainwashing my child. Every day Aubrey came home from school with a printed label stuck to her shirt as she recited by heart her daily PTA pledge, "Momma, let's go to Chick-fil-A on Wednesday, October seventh, to have a milkshake with the principal. Everyone can go, grown-ups AND kids! We don't have to eat dinner there; we can just go for dessert!"

"No, Aubrey," I answered as she began to cry because everyone was going.

"Momma, let's go to Cici's Pizza on Thursday, October eighth, for Spirit Night! All proceeds benefit Belle Hall Elementary!"

"No, Aubrey," I answered as she began to cry because everyone was going.

"Momma, if I sell ten packages of wrapping paper, I can win a fabulous prize!"

Not only did my child come home from school every day with a sticker on her chest and a memorized monologue, but the school invested in one of those annoying machines that called you, then asked you to "hold for an important message." If it was that important, I felt sure that an actual person would call me.

PTA people, stop this! This instant! My child goes to public school for a reason! If I could afford to take a family of five out to dinner every night and had friends who didn't buy all their wrapping paper half price at Kmart after Christmas every year, my kids would go to private school. And how am I supposed to get three kids dressed and out the door by 6:30 to get in line for the Spirit Night buffet at Cici's Pizza if you won't stop calling me? So stop it. Now.

I mean for the love, I just sold fifteen lobsters in the middle of a recession. Oh, you don't have to go back and read that last sentence again—you read it right the first time . . . LOBSTERS. I sold fifteen lobsters in the midst of the worst economic climate since the Great Depression. For $12.50 a pop.

I'll give credit where credit is due. The lobsters were a pretty good idea. We had a lobster party with a bunch of our friends: everyone bought their own lobster, I cooked side dishes, and we had a great time. But I'm not asking anybody to pay $9.99 for a four-by-four square of foil wrapping paper.

My sister taught second grade in Alabama, and her PTA was smart; they gave you the option of volunteering or writing a check for fifty dollars. Sign me up. I'd pay the PTA fifty dollars to quit programming my child to peddle their wares on the streets of Mount Pleasant for some stupid plastic monkey that I could buy her for a buck at any Dollar General—but NO. She didn't want my crap; she wanted their crap, and she wanted to earn it. What kind of values are they trying to teach our kids, anyway?

24

. . . .

She Works Hard for the Money

As my children have gotten older, I have realized I must teach them the value of a dollar and instill in them a strong work ethic. No child of mine is going to be walking around with a sense of entitlement. No way. No how. Even if it means I have to say no nine times out of ten and make them work their way through preschool, flipping burgers at Burger King. My children will learn to value a dollar and the satisfaction that can only be gained through hard work and perseverance. But, well . . . it's a process.

At first, I tried to praise and reward good behavior, but this usually just lead to Aubrey asking me for something every time she picked up a toy. The upside of this particular method was that every time I cleaned the house, I had two little cheerleaders who followed me around saying, "Dat's such a good job, Mommy! You ah such a big gull!" And when they came home from preschool to a spotless house, they would occasionally say, "Oh, Momma! Thank you sooo much for cleaning my house!" Their house? What? Last time I checked, my last name was not Gosselin. This is my house; they only live here. Apparently, it was time to reevaluate.

I realized the tactics I was employing left something to be desired, so when Aubrey was four years old, we instituted an allowance system. Aubrey could earn a dollar a day for obedience, good behavior, and cleaning up after herself without being told. Obedience is a pretty all-encompassing rule for a preschooler. It included everything from putting her dishes in the sink and placing her shoes on the shelf by the front door to stopping the very first time I told her to leave her sister alone.

The idea was that she would do her "chores" and follow the rules, and hopefully by the end of the week she would have seven dollars. (Who am I kidding, right?) We would save 10 percent, give 10 percent to our church, and the rest could be used at her discretion.

Her first week on this system was extremely effective. She "yes ma'amed" until she was blue in the face and was busy all day long looking for something to clean or some way to help me. I paid her in change, at her request (she prefers "the little metal monies" to cold hard cash), and at the end of the week, we sat down to count it all up.

After counting everything in her piggy bank, including stray coins she had picked up around the house, she had a little over six dollars. In the past, Aubrey had always been so excited about taking money with her to church and seemed to understand that somehow her money was going to benefit someone other than herself.

"All right, Aubrey, it looks like you have about sixty-five cents you need to take to church tomorrow," I told her.

She was horrified. Her chin began to tremble, and her eyes

filled with tears as she exclaimed, "But Momma, this is MY money, and I don't want to give it to God!"

"Hold on a second," I said as I quickly pulled sixty-five cents out of her pile of coins. I made a small stack with "God's money" and a large one with hers.

"This is your money," I said, pointing to the larger pile. "And THIS is God's money." I gestured toward the small stack of coins.

"OH!" She giggled because she was so relieved. "I guess He can have a little more," she said as she kicked in an extra six cents.

As she got older, the temptation of doing what she wanted to do, when she wanted to do it, began to outweigh the promise of a dollar at the end of a day, and Aubrey hit a dry spell. The economy was bad, and my four-year-old was feeling it in her pink Disney princess pocketbook. It took her about a month to collect eight dollars, and it was burning a hole in her pocket.

I was excited to take her to the store so she could see how far her money would actually stretch and tried not to smile too broadly as I told her that eight dollars would not be enough to buy the Barbie House-o'-Skanks or Barbie's Skank-Mobile.

We moved to a section of toys that were within her budget, and, shock of all shocks, she chose yet another Barbie doll to add to her already-extensive collection. I assured her that she had plenty of money to buy it, and we made our way to the register.

She placed the Barbie on the turnstile and held her wallet in her still chubby baby fingers. The cashier gave us the total and I said, "Okay, honey, time to fork it over."

Aubrey reached in her wallet and grabbed a handful of cash and coins and placed them in my hands, with her strawberry-blond eyebrows raised, leaving several dollars behind.

"Nope, I gotta have all of it," I told her.

She turned her pink princess wallet upside down on the turnstile, then turned to me with a scowl and said, "That's IT! It's all gone." I couldn't have said it better myself.

I thought after spending some of her own allowance, Aubrey was starting to appreciate what it meant to work for your money. As far as my husband went, she seemed to understand that her daddy's job is to build "hostables" (hospitals). Aubrey and Emma both love going to visit their daddy at his work on occasion. They love to play with the women who work in the office and choose a piece of candy out of the huge bowl in the reception area. They leave feeling like they are ten feet tall and somebody.

My job was a bit more complicated in Aubrey's little mind. I was working one morning, which means I was typing away on my laptop, in my pajamas, with no makeup on and stopping whenever I needed to play with or discipline my children. I was taking a break from writing to feed my kids and casually asked Aubrey as I made sandwiches, "What is Mommy's job?"

"Ummm, puttin' my sister in time-out . . ."

I laughed. "What else?"

"Writing books."

I was a little impressed. I was, in fact, working on my first book and writing a weekly column for *The Moultrie News* in Mount Pleasant, South Carolina.

"What kind of books?" I asked just to see what she would say.

"Facebooks." I went from being impressed she knew what I did to being horrified, again, that she actually knew what I did.

At the mention of her future career as a Facebooker for the second time in less than a month, I began to realize my children's concept of work wasn't exactly accurate. Aubrey understood that her mommy and daddy had jobs, but the nature of the actual work continued to be a subject matter beyond her understanding. Her little mind just couldn't comprehend exactly what it was that her parents did to put food on the table.

Aubrey was sitting by the front door one evening waiting for her daddy to get home from work and play with her when she looked at me and asked impatiently, "Momma, where my daddy is?"

"He's at work, baby. He'll be home in just a little while. Daddy works so hard for us so we can stay home and be together."

"Yeah," she replied in her most mature voice, "him is just at work chewin' gum and eatin' candy . . ."

Apparently, I still have some work to do.

25

. . . .

Sweet Dreams

The predictability and comfort of a bedtime routine is as important to parents as it is to their children. After a hectic day of disciplining your children and being busy doing whatever it is your life requires of you, it feels good to settle your children in their nice warm beds at night and reassure them of your love and adoration. That's the idea, anyway.

Bedtime at my house often brings to mind trying to force a pack of rabid dogs into a single cage. My children, exhausted and desperate for sleep, will do whatever it takes to prolong the process of going to bed as long as humanly possible. Because of this we have a routine that starts a full hour before their actual bedtime to make the transition from playtime to sleep time a predictable and comforting process.

We usually start with a bath, regardless of whether or not they need it. Aubrey and Emma love to get in the bathtub and play with their tub toys, have pretend tea parties, and generally make a gigantic mess for my husband and me to clean up, but it's a good way to signal to them that bedtime is coming.

Of course, bath time at my house isn't always calm, soothing, and drama-free, and it has ended more than once with me bleaching the bathtub. Thankfully, Emma's days of pooping in the bathtub were short-lived, but Aubrey still gets nervous and bails out whenever her little sister breaks wind in the tub. I can't blame her; we've both seen the "floaters" of her past.

In addition to actually getting clean and calming down before going to bed, during bath time the girls can bond and discuss the day's events with one another. But more often than not it is another time for me to act as a mediator between two stubborn little girls.

One evening, the girls were enjoying a soak in the tub when Emma began yelling in her "OOOOOH, my sister did something bad and I'm going to get her in trouble" voice.

"MOMMA, MOMMA, MOMMA!"

I went running into the bathroom to see what the problem was.

"Aub-a-rey said 'too-pid'!"

I looked at Aubrey as she looked everywhere but at my face.

"Aubrey, did you say 'stupid'?" I asked her.

"I didn't! I didn't, Momma! I REALLY didn't. I'm not even lying!"

Emma reassured me. "Her did, Momma! Her said 'too-pid'!"

"Aubrey . . ." I prodded.

"I didn't, Momma! I said 'upid-stay.' Repeat after me, Momma: 'uh-uh-upid-stay.' SpongeBob says it!"

Pig Latin . . . at four years old? Really? I have a hard enough time understanding them when they are speaking English without the addition of the secret language of prepubescent boys across the country. Even though I was a little smug that I had a bilingual child, I heaved a big sigh and explained. "Aubrey, 'upid-stay' IS the same thing as saying 'stupid,' and SpongeBob says a lot of things we shouldn't say. Okay? Time to get out of the tub."

Aubrey hopped right out and began to get ready for bed, but Emma wanted to continue to soak in the bathtub.

"Emma, honey, you have to get out."

"I not weady yep, Momma. I not."

"Honey, you have to get out."

"Oh, I just do dis den, Momma," she said as she pushed up on her hands and toes, sticking her tiny little booty straight up in the air. She was in a downward-dog position, with most of her body out of the water.

"What are you doing?" I asked her, a little confused.

"I'm out of da tub, Momma!" She grinned. She was so proud of her own ingenuity.

I tried to convince her that it was bedtime and that, regardless of how she was positioned in the tub, it was simply time to get out. She was eventually persuaded by the promise of reading books and climbed out of the bath to join her sister in their shared bedroom.

Story time is another time that can be so precious, sweet, and thoroughly exhausting. Now, I love books. I love to read, and I want my kids to love it as well, but something about reading out loud to my children makes me yawn like somebody slipped a roofie into my Mommy Juice. I can be wide awake, and as soon as I start to read, I'll have to stop every minute or two to yawn.

Because I get so sleepy when I'm reading out loud, I like to keep bedtime books short and sweet. I'm a *Goodnight Moon* kind of girl. "Goodnight stars. Goodnight air. Goodnight noises everywhere." The end.

But, as I said, my children like to prolong the bedtime routine as long as possible and usually bring me a book that is the equivalent of reading the King James Version of the Bible or *The Canterbury Tales* . . . in the original Middle English.

On this particular night, Aubrey chose *Froggy Goes Out to Eat.* I thought I would be sneaky and leave out some of the zany and fun sound effects that are conveniently written into the story. I was tired and just not in the mood to read aloud words that sounded like they came right out of a Marvel comic. "ZING. ZANG. ZUP. ZWIP. BANG. SMACK. CRACK."

I left out the sound effects and read on for about fifteen seconds before Aubrey completely and totally busted me.

"MOMMA!" she protested. "You skipped these words . . . BANG. SMACK. CRACK! Do it again, and do it RIGHT!"

I sighed and started over. As I read, I was continually distracted by my youngest, Sadie, crying from the next room. I paused once to yell some suggestions into the living room to my husband to try to help him ease her to sleep while continuing to read to the big girls. We neared the end of the book, and Sadie was still crying. Emma cupped her tiny little fingers around her mouth and yelled into the living room. "DADDY! GIVE HER SOME MILKS IN HER BOTTLE! AND PUT HER IN DA BED. HER IS SWEEPY! 'KAY?"

Aubrey and I collapsed on the bed laughing at the three-year-old yelling at her daddy how to take care of her baby sister. Emma glared at us. " 'Top lappin', guys. It not punny!"

"DADDY, DON'T PORGET HER SASSY AND HER BWANKY! 'KAY?" She turned to me, her mission now accomplished, and said, "You can pinish weading now, Momma."

After reading a bedtime story—or oftentimes instead of reading—we will turn out the lights and play a game the girls

call "Wet's caulk about our dweams." (This has nothing to do
with Sheetrock but is a game I developed to keep Aubrey from
talking about nightmares and scary stuff she doesn't want to
dream about right before bedtime, usually prolonging bedtime
even further.)

Emma loves to be in charge of this exercise and will start by
asking, "What you gonna dweam about tonight, Momma?" I
try to make up something as silly as possible to get a good laugh
out of them (hard to believe, I'm sure). Then Emma will continue
to make her rounds by asking, "Sissy, wha' you gonna dweam
about?"

Aubrey's answers usually have to do with mermaids and/or
junk food. That's just who she is. Emma's dreams usually in-
volve going to the beach with Shuggie or hanging out with "the
farm people," which is how my children collectively and lovingly refer to all of my in-laws.

After a story, talking about our dreams, and finally, finally
getting tucked into bed, it's time to say our prayers. Saying our
prayers must be the very last thing we do every night. My children apparently have a lot to be thankful for and are careful not
to forget a single thing as they pray.

By this point in the evening, not only am I ready for a shower
and sleep, but I am ready to spend some time with my husband
and Sadie before they both go to sleep as well.

The girls are very strict about my hands being folded a certain
way and my eyes being closed before they begin, but apparently
these rules only apply to me, because they will stop in a heartbeat,
right in the middle of a sweet and sincere conversation with
Jesus to yell, "CWOSE you eyes, Momma!"

Once we are all following their rules, Emma will begin,
"Deah World, Fank you for my fam-i-wee, fank you for my

sis-tohs, fank you for my best fwiend ever in da whole world, Poppa. Fank you 'Mary had a wittle wamb.'"

On this particular night, I thought I could wrap this up if we were praying for Mary's lamb. I said, "AMEN!"

Emma's eyes popped open, and she pointed her tiny little finger in my face. "No, I not done yep. Cwose you eyes, Momma." She folded her hands again as she continued, "Fank you for the farm, fank you for my cousins, fank you for Shuggie and waffles . . ."

She paused to take a breath, and I took the opportunity to blurt out another "Amen." She pointed her finger in my face again and scowled at me. "NO, I NOT DONE YEP! Do dis, Momma," she said as she showed me once again how to fold my hands. "Fank you for da Lord, thank you the stars and the trees."

Wow. That was a new one, thanking God for . . . God.

"Emma," I said, risking her finger in my face by interrupting her again. "You know you can talk to God all by yourself when Mommy's not in here, right?"

Her hands spread in amazement, and her mouth and eyes were wide open. "OH MY GASH!"

"You keep talking, baby, and He'll keep listening. Mommy has to go to bed!"

Thankfully, for all of us, God doesn't need eight hours of sleep and two cups of Starbucks Café Verona before He can keep up with you all day tomorrow.

Boys Have a Penis

And girls have a coo-coo. That's what the girls at my house have, anyway. I realize there has been all manner of research done about teaching your children the correct names for their, ahem, parts—and how by saying "penis" and "vagina" to your children, somehow they will be closer to you and realize how open and accepting you are of their sexuality. Hell, I even saw one mother on *Oprah* say the word "clitoris" to her ten-year-old. But, Lord help me, I cannot say "vagina" to my daughters.

I tried. I really did. I had a professor in college who had me convinced if I would only say "vagina" all my worries about my daughters being sexually promiscuous or turning into a Lifetime movie would magically disappear.

This seemed like a great theory until I actually had to say the word "vagina" to my own child. I don't remember exactly how the conversation came up, but I do remember feeling like a complete and total pervert. It didn't help matters that as soon as the word was out of my mouth, she began chanting, "bagina-bagina-bagina-bagina-bagina."

"Oops," I thought. "I have made a big mistake—quite possibly a huge mistake. She is going to go to preschool tomorrow and tell everyone she sees that she has a vagina."

Maybe you live in a liberal big city where the teacher would smile and nod approvingly at your openness as a mother. But I don't. I live in the Deep South, where even women in their thirties with three kids pray their parents think they are still virgins. I had to fix this. Now.

I started scrambling to cover my tracks. I started thinking of every acceptable nickname I could for the old "va-jay-jay," just to try to distract her from her new favorite word.

"Va-jay-jay, Aubrey. You can call it a va-jay-jay. Or pee-pee!" I frantically tried to find a substitute.

"Bagina-bagina-BAGINA," she chanted.

"Or, or a cookie! You can call it a cookie!"

"NO! Momma! You not eat it!" She squealed and giggled. This was not a point I was willing to argue.

"Coo-coo, Aubrey. It's called your coo-coo!" And thus the coo-coo was born at our house.

The penis conversation came along only a few short weeks later, when Aubrey saw her daddy peeing in the bathroom.

"You an ele-pant, Daddy?" she asked. "Momma, that Daddy's coo-coo?"

I cringed all the way down to my momma's Southern Baptist roots as I said, "No, baby." (Sigh.) "That is his penis."

"Oh, he have a long coo-coo, Momma?"

"Yes, baby," I answered her, already trying to think of a way to change the subject. It wasn't necessary. She wasn't very excited about the word "penis." Smart girl . . . or so it seemed for a couple of years.

By the time Aubrey was four, she had a newfound interest in all things genitalia. Every bath time was peppered with questions about her own body and anyone else she could think to ask about. I used the opportunity to remind her that her body was hers, that it was private and she shouldn't show it to anyone else, and that if anyone tried to look at her coo-coo or touch it, she should always tell me.

My husband tried to avoid being naked in front of the girls at all costs, to hopefully decrease some of their ever-growing interest. But from time to time we found ourselves discussing penises with our preschool daughters.

On Aubrey's last day of preschool, we were all dressed and ready for school, so I let the girls watch *SpongeBob* until it was time to go. As I was checking my e-mail, I overheard Aubrey say, "I hope HE doesn't have a penis."

I heard brakes squealing. Lord, have mercy.

"Aubrey, come here!"

Aubrey walked toward me with a little sideways grin. "What?"

"What did you just say?"

We were about to leave for her very last day of preschool, ever, and I didn't want to remember this day as "the day Aubrey told her classmates about SpongeBob's penis."

Aubrey began giggling uncontrollably. "Hee-hee, penis."

"Do you know what that is?"

She actually snorted she was laughing so hard. "Yep, it's a boy's coo-coo."

Sigh.

"That's right, but it's private (Hello World!), and we don't talk about it at school."

Aubrey was still snickering as she walked back into the living room. "'Kay, Momma."

We made it through the last day of school, and I thought we were safe. I mean, I have three girls; surely we could let the penis conversation rest for a bit.

A few weeks later, one of my best friends, Sara, needed some help watching her four-year-old son while she and her hubby snuck off for their anniversary. I was glad to help, because she is one of my favorite people in the universe. The girl has more energy than anyone I've ever met, and every time she comes to my house, it is always clean when she leaves and all my kids have been bathed. I don't actually understand how she does it, but I love her so much, I'd do just about anything for her.

Her son, Tristan, is every bit as sweet as his momma, and both Aubrey and Emma claim him as their best friend. His parents are raising him to be a true gentleman by making him open doors for my little girls and assist them in pulling their bicycles out of ditches and by making him stay out of the girls' way when they are changing clothes or using the restroom. The kids are really quite funny about it, slamming doors in each other's faces and yelling, "Excuse me, I meed some pwivacy!"

But because Aubrey had been so inquisitive about all things genitalia lately, my Mommy Radar was on high alert for any hanky-panky of the preschool persuasion. It rained nonstop on one of the days Tristan spent with us, which led to lots of fort building and movie watching.

It was late in the afternoon; Aubrey, Emma, and Tristan were lined up on a pallet on the floor, snuggled up together watching a movie. I was in the kitchen starting dinner when I heard some mischievous giggles coming from the living room. I immediately expected the worst and tried to sneak around the corner to spy on them and catch them in the act of "I'll Show You Mine, You Show Me Yours," but to no avail. Every time I popped my head around a corner, Aubrey and Tristan would be staring at the TV, trying to look innocent, while Emma snoozed beside them, oblivious.

We continued this cat-and-mouse game for about fifteen minutes, at which point Emma had fallen asleep. I picked her up and put her in between Aubrey and Tristan to separate them; if I couldn't catch them in the act, it was the best I could do.

Several days after Tristan's parents returned from their trip, Aubrey walked into my bathroom while I was taking a bath and began yet another drawn-out conversation on her favorite topic.

"Mommy, why your coo-coo not look like mines?"

"Because I'm a grown-up, Aubrey. Kids and grown-ups don't look the same."

"Oh, you have a grown-up coo-coo, and Daddy has a grown-up penis. Right, Momma?"

"Yes, baby . . ." I closed my eyes and leaned my head against the wall, mentally willing this conversation to end.

"Not like Tristan. He just has a LITTLE, TINY, kid-sized penis!"

"WHAT?" I screeched. I sat up so quickly that water splashed over the side of the tub.

Her eyes widened in shock as she realized she had just busted herself. I could see her gears turning as she quickly tried to manage damage control.

"Aubrey, how do you know what Tristan's penis looks like? Did he show it to you?"

She bit her bottom lip and wrinkled her nose and forehead. "Welllllll, I think so."

"What do you mean, you think so? Did you show him your coo-coo?"

She nervously pulled at her curls and twisted her hands together. "Ummmm . . . maybe just a little bit. I did . . . but Momma, Daddy has a big, long, grown-up penis, and Tristan just has a LITTLE kid-sized one like this . . ." She held up her left hand in front of her left eye in an okay sign and squinted through the eraser-sized hole in her fingers. "It's just this big, Momma."

I felt part of my large intestine herniate as I swallowed my laughter. I sternly discussed with her, again, how her body is hers, it is private, and we are not supposed to be showing it to folks—especially boys. I called Tristan's mom, so she could talk to him, and prayed fervently that our obsession with all things penile was over.

At bedtime about a week later, I was lying in Aubrey and Emma's bedroom, and we were saying our prayers and making up silly stories when Emma busted out with, "Momma, I hab one, two, free nuts!" She unfolded three fingers as she counted them out.

Aubrey began giggling uncontrollably.

Oh, Sweet, Sweet Lord in Heaven. Not Emma, too.

"You have three WHAT?" I was nervous. Really, really nervous.

"NUTS, Momma, I SAID." She leaned forward to scream in my face, "I HAB FREE NUTS!"

Aubrey couldn't even open her eyes and was lying curled on her side, in the fetal position, and holding her stomach, she was laughing so hard.

Emma jumped off the bed and went running out of the room to tell her daddy that she had "free nuts."

I was so scared to ask the most obvious question, but I'm their momma, and it had to be done . . . "Aubrey, what is a nut?"

"Sumpin' a squirrel eats, Momma!!!" She squealed and continued to laugh hysterically. "Emma is SOOOO silly!"

I took a deep, cleansing breath before replying, "Yes. Yes, she is."

27

·······

Here Comes the Bride's Worst

Nightmare

Being a flower girl is a rite of passage in every little girl's life. When Bebo, my younger brother, proposed to his girlfriend, Anna, they asked all three of my daughters to be flower girls. They were over the moon with excitement; I, on the other hand, was a complete and total nervous wreck.

I mean, you've been reading about my kids. You know my kids. I had a lot of reasons to be nervous. There were eight flower girls in the wedding. Bebo and Anna had asked all of their nieces (who could walk) to participate, and with that many children involved, someone was bound to screw something up. I had fifty bucks riding on one of my kids.

My brother and his wife were more than gracious and assured me repeatedly that if one or more of my children decided to bail at the last minute, it would be fine. Which was very kind of them—but I wasn't worried about my children deciding not to walk down the aisle. I was terrified to think of what they were going to do as they walked down the aisle.

In the weeks before the wedding, we spent countless hours covering proper flower-girl etiquette: keep your hands to yourself, walk slowly, don't throw your flowers or your basket at anyone, and stand quietly beside Mommy. On our way to the rehearsal, we reviewed flower-girl protocol, and Aubrey and Emma recited the rules by heart. They followed the rules, but I soon learned that there were a few areas of concern that I hadn't accounted for.

The wedding was held at Children's Harbor on Lake Martin in Alabama. The wedding party was standing at a point overlooking the lake and facing toward the cutest little chapel you've ever seen. As we began our first run-through of the service, I braced myself for unprecedented O'Bryant behavior. I knew it was going to be bad. I just didn't know how bad.

Aubrey walked down the aisle, keeping her hands to herself and her head up as she walked right past the wedding party and the minister to the shore of the lake, where she began picking up boulders and throwing them into the lake. I don't mean skipping small stones—she had to use both hands and lift with her legs to throw them in the lake with a loud "KERPLUNK!"

Emma walked down the aisle, holding her crotch à la Michael Jackson (hee-hee) the entire way. She did not follow her sister to the water's edge at first but came and stood beside me just as she had been instructed—for about thirty seconds. At which point she lifted my knee-length dress over her head and up to my bra. I grabbed my dress, shoved it down in a panic, and looked up just in time to see the father of the bride doubled over with laughter and pointing me out to a few other family members.

As I was scolding Emma, I heard my sister exclaim, "Oh, Aubrey! NO!" I turned around just in time to see Aubrey picking up a piece of neon-green chewing gum off a rock at the shoreline. It had already been chewed and was melted in the summer sun. She stretched it up toward her, and the gum spun into a long, stringy, sticky comet. I rushed to her side to help her before it wrapped itself around her in the wind, and as I picked the threads of gum off of her hand, Aubrey decided to "help" me by biting and licking off stray spots of someone else's gum.

The bridesmaids, bless their young and childless hearts, kept saying over and over, "They are so cute! Aw, how precious!" If seeing my children at the wedding rehearsal wasn't good enough birth control for these girls, I'm pretty sure they are beyond all help.

We spent the evening vigorously cramming for the next day's events.

"Emma, are you going to play in the lake tomorrow?" I asked in my best you'd-better-answer-me-right-now mommy voice.

"No, Momma. I not."

"Are you going to throw rocks in the lake?"

"Yip, I will, Momma."

"WHAT DID YOU SAY?"

She giggled and covered her hand with her mouth. "I jest kidding, Momma! I not frow wocks. I not. I dwop my petals and stand wichu and dat's all, Momma."

I turned to Aubrey and asked, "What are you going to do tomorrow?"

"I'll walk down the aisle veeerrry slow-ly, and drop my pet-als veeeeerry gent-ly."

"That's right!"

We went through our game plan over, and over, and over again. It was bad enough that the Big Berthas were almost spilling out of my bridesmaid's dress. You could basically see every-thing but my actual zipple, and my Spanx were cutting off my circulation. It was going to be all I could do at the wedding to keep my bra and the Berthas inside my dress, suck it in, and stand on a grassy incline in heels. The very last thing I needed at this wedding was to have to fish one of my kids out of the lake.

We had brunch in honor of Bebo and Anna the day of the wedding, and I dressed the girls in matching pink seersucker dresses. As we walked to the clubhouse on the resort where we were staying, I once again admonished the girls to be on their best behavior.

"What is brunch, Momma?" Aubrey asked.

"It's a very fancy breakfast."

"Oooooh, like Fancy Nancy?"

"JUST like that! We have to use our fanciest manners."

They were perfect. Little angels in seersucker and hair bows. They put their linen napkins in their laps, said "please" and "thank you," and Aubrey even scolded my mother once, saying, "SHUG-GIE! Don't talk with food in your mouth."

I was impressed . . . and scared chitless. Because I knew these were not my children and that at any minute we could begin a downward spiral that would end in certain death—or at least in me having to leave the wedding in the middle of the ceremony to take one or both of them back to our villa.

Inevitably, one of the girls had to use the potty, so I rounded up my herd and headed to the ladies' room. There were two stalls, so I sent Aubrey into one and Emma into the other and waited for them to finish. When Aubrey was finished, I went in to use the restroom myself, leaving the stall door cracked so I could keep an eye on them.

Aubrey was washing her hands when Emma came out of her stall. Emma could reach the soap, but she was too short to get her hands underneath the water faucet.

"Aubrey," I said. "Pick Emma up and help her wash her hands."

Aubrey started to reach around Emma's waist to give her a boost, and Emma freaked out.

"NOOOOOOOOO! I DO IT BY MYSELF!" she screamed.

"Just put her down, Aubrey. I'll help her in a second." I sighed.

Aubrey curled up into a ball at the base of the sink and looked up at Emma from her fetal position on the floor and said sweetly, "Here you go, Emma. You can just step on my back. Go ahead, step on me."

I watched in amazement as Emma giggled and stepped onto Aubrey's seersuckered back to rinse her hands. I took this unprecedented display of sisterly love and teamwork as a good omen. Maybe, maybe, I wasn't going to be completely humiliated at the wedding.

If I was nervous before the rehearsal, I was close to needing to breathe into a paper sack before the wedding. I continued to review the Flower Girl Rules with a few additions: no doing the pee-pee dance down the aisle, no playing with someone else's chewing gum, no throwing boulders into the lake, and please, please for the love of everything that is good and holy, no showing the wedding guests Mommy's underwear.

I wondered if a member of the bride's family might have slipped a sedative into the girls' orange juice at brunch, because their performance at the wedding went off without a hitch. No rocks, no gum, and (there is a God in heaven) no flashing my Britney at the wedding guests.

28

. . . .

I Swear to Tell The Truth

Where exactly does a parent draw the line when teaching their children to tell The Truth? Is it enough to expect them to cough it up when they have bitten a sibling or taken something that doesn't belong to them? How do we teach our children that while it's important not to lie, sometimes The Truth isn't always the nicest or best thing to say? Because my kids need to learn this lesson—the sooner, the better.

I've been asked more than once by a child, "Did they get all the babies out of your tummy?" And that kind of thing is to be expected. I spent nine months telling you I was pregnant, I gained enough weight to look like I was having triplets, and all I have to show for it is a six-pound, fourteen-ounce baby and a still-fat stomach. I can't be offended by that kind of honesty.

The kind of honesty I'm referring to has more to do with The Truth that offends. Like the time Aubrey and I were at Wal-Mart and saw a woman with three inches of white roots, jet-black hair that extended another two inches, and every hair on her head sticking straight up. Aubrey yelled across the store, "WOOK, Mommy! It's Cwuella De'bille!"

Trust me when I say that nothing was lost in toddler translation and that everyone within a twenty-foot radius knew exactly who and what my child was talking about. And she did look like Cruella De Vil—all she needed was a fur coat and a Virginia Slim in a red cigarette holder. And judging from the look she gave me and Aubrey, she was thinking about skinning us both.

There are some facts that simply do not need to be spoken aloud. As we all learned growing up, "If you don't have anything nice to say, then don't say anything at all." While true, it's an aphorism that is totally lost on toddlers.

Emma once climbed into bed with me while it was still dark outside and woke me from my slumber by pinching my nostrils closed and thereby cutting off my air supply. Not the most pleasant way to wake up, but I thought I was being a really good sport and going with the flow when, instead of flinging her into the floor as my endorphins kicked in and caused me to fight for survival, I made a "HOOOONK" noise worthy of a Jim Henson Muppet. She felt somewhat differently.

"EWWWWWW! Mommy, your breaf stinks! You been frowin' up, Momma?"

Actually, no. As you may have noticed from my supine position, closed eyes, and deep, even breathing, you little devil child, I wasn't vomiting. I was sleeping.

When we moved from Georgia to South Carolina, Aubrey was three. Nobody in our family smokes, and she had never seen someone smoking a cigarette before. It just so happened that some of our neighbors were smokers, and it never really crossed my mind to address the issue with Aubrey.

Until one day I saw her pick up a toothpick between her index and middle fingers and suck on it like it was a Kool menthol. She took the toothpick out of her mouth, and while it dangled between her fingers, Aubrey puckered up her lips and blew out a stream of imaginary smoke.

"Aubrey. WHAT are you doing?"

"Oh, it's okay, Momma. I'ne just smokin'."

"NO. It is NOT OKAY! Smoking is so bad for you, Aubrey. It is nasty and disgusting. It will make you REALLY, REALLY sick. You would have to go to the doctor all the time and get lots of shots! Do you understand?"

"I unner-stan, Momma."

The very next day, we were playing in the front yard when one of our precious neighbors wandered over to visit with a cigarette in her hand.

Aubrey didn't even say "hello."

"My momma said smoking is nasty and bisgusting and you need to stop."

I was mortified. Obviously, anyone who can read and smokes knows it's bad for them. But I didn't really want my new neighbors thinking I was sitting in my house telling my toddler how disgusting they were.

A few days later, I caught Aubrey once again puckering up her lips and pretending to blow smoke out of her mouth. I gave her the Momma Stink-Eye and said, "What do you think you're doing?"

"Oh! Don't worry, Momma. I quit smoking."

How do I teach them that there are degrees of Truth? And that full disclosure isn't always in their best interest without teaching them to lie to me?

Aubrey takes every opportunity to point out the differences in our bodies. It's gotten to the point that I feel the need to run and cover myself if she so much as walks into the room when I'm changing. I am well aware of my body's flaws and do not need her help in pointing them out.

After a stomach virus tore through our house and our digestive systems for over two weeks, I was once again tucking the big girls into bed. I was lying on Emma's bed with my legs hanging off, and Aubrey was standing between my legs, explaining to me all the reasons *Purplicious* is far superior to *Pinkalicious*. She ran her hand up my calf briefly, while talking, and immediately said, "GROSS! Momma, you need to shave."

I thought, "Thank you, once again, small person, for stating the completely obvious. I have realized for the last two weeks that I needed to shave, but I was busy bringing you Popsicles and Sprite and cleaning up your bodily fluids all over the house. I was going to shave, but when I went to bed last night at 2:00 A.M., I just wasn't in the mood. Then your sister woke me up at 5:00 A.M., and for some odd reason, despite my three full hours of sleep, I still didn't feel like it. I thought about shaving after washing all the sheets in the house for the third time in three days, but once again chose taking care of you and your sisters over the hair on my legs. Now the hair on my legs has crossed the line from short and stubbly to long, soft, and flowing. I realize I either need to shave or quit wearing short pants and start using patchouli oil instead of deodorant, but for now, if it's all right with you, I think I'll just finish reading you a bedtime story."

But instead of speaking my mind, I simply agreed with her. "Mmm-hmm. You're right. I need to shave."

Because I want my children to be honest with me. I want them to feel like they are able to tell me anything without fearing the consequences while still teaching them that negative actions have negative consequences.

My husband was tucking Aubrey into bed one evening, and as he kissed her goodnight, she looked up at him and said, "Daddy, I would never throw a beer bottle in the street like Emma did." He was confused and asked her what she was talking about, but she just kept repeating herself.

His confusion ended when he walked out our front door a few minutes after putting Aubrey in bed and found a beer bottle smashed to bits on the driveway. I had been cleaning out a cooler from a recent neighborhood get-together and had lined up all the leftover drinks by our front door, thinking I would put them away later. Apparently, those full bottles of beer looked just like water balloons to Aubrey.

Zeb came into our bathroom, where I was soaking in the bathtub and trying to relax, and said, "So where did Emma get a beer bottle to throw in the driveway? There is busted glass everywhere."

"What are you talking about?" I asked.

He explained Aubrey's bedtime story to me, and I interrupted. "Aubrey did it."

"Well, she said Emma did it."

"Anytime Aubrey starts a sentence with 'I would never,' it means she already HAS."

He was skeptical. Emma has traditionally been the child who could look you straight in the eye and lie to you, while Aubrey is much more melodramatic and will regularly confess to her crimes before you even realize she's done anything wrong—usually with one hand clutching her heart while large tears well up in her blue eyes. She will solemnly say, "I can't tell a wie, Momma. I did it! I'm the one who ate the cake! It was me!" But Aubrey had recently been blaming her sister for crimes she committed on her own.

The following morning over breakfast, when I asked Emma if she had thrown a bottle in the driveway, she was completely and totally confounded. She didn't even deny it; she just looked at me like I had lost my mind.

Aubrey couldn't take the heat of her sister being wrongly accused. She threw her hand over her heart and, clutching her cereal spoon like a microphone, gave me a confession so thorough, Detectives Benson and Stabler would have been high-fiving each other in the interrogation room.

I never doubted that Aubrey was guilty but used the opportunity to explain to her again how important it is to tell the truth. It is one of the many paradoxes we find ourselves in as parents: How do we make our children understand the truth is important if we tell white lies in front of them? How do we teach them to censor their thoughts in public but to bare their souls at home? How do we help them to distinguish between keeping secrets for the good of others and keeping secrets from us that can potentially hurt them or someone else?

I don't know the answers to these questions. I'm pretty sure answering them is what being a parent is all about, and maybe in the next eighteen years I'll learn a little something to help my children and me survive their childhoods and adolescences with grace. I'm just hoping the amount of beer and cigarettes involved so far is no indication of what's to come.

Love and Marriage

As Aubrey neared her fifth birthday, she became bewitched with all things involving love, princesses, and marriage. She began speaking on a regular basis about growing up, getting married, and having babies (the first of whom she plans to name Angelina Ballerina, and the second Japan Ursula Wiley).

Toward the end of the school year, she began talking about a boy named Christian nonstop. Christian this, Christian that.

"Momma, Christian is sooooo ham-some, and I'ne going to marry him instead of Mr. Jerry." One of cur neighbors who had apparently proposed to her.

"Momma, Christian is so sweet to me," she would say with a sparkle in her eyes and a smile on her face.

"Aubrey, where did you meet him? Does he go to your school? Does he come to the nursery at church?"

She became frustrated and yelled, "YOU KNOW . . . CHRISTIAN!"

"No, baby, Mommy doesn't know him."

And I really didn't. I scoured my brain for all the places we went: the gym, Bible study group, church, school. I had no idea who this kid was, and Aubrey was as enamored with him as she was disgusted with me for not knowing who he was.

This dialogue went on for days on end. She talked about how wonderful Christian was, and I quizzed her relentlessly, trying to figure out the identity of my future son-in-law.

Until one day she finally snapped and screamed at me, "Momma, you said I was gonna marry him! REMEMBER?"

I had a sudden flashback and a moment of complete clarity as I remembered our conversation the night she had sashayed in the door and announced proudly, "I'm going to marry Mr. Jerry!"

Mr. Jerry was our neighbor—I won't speculate as to his exact age, but he has a headful of gray hair and grandchildren. Neither of these facts matters to Aubrey; all she cares about is his chocolate Lab Belle and the fact that if she married him, she would have her very own dog.

My husband objected vehemently. "You CANNOT marry Mr. Jerry. He is way too old for you."

"Well, I guess I'll just marry my daddy then," she speculated.

"You can't marry your daddy, because he's your daddy and I'm already married to him," I explained as she climbed into her bed.

"But who will I marry, Momma?" She raised her eyebrows as if she was already worried about becoming an old maid. I lay down beside her in bed as I said, "I don't know his name, but I'm sure he will be a Christian"—here's my moment of clarity—"and handsome and very sweet to you . . ."

I was snapped out of my reverie by my own laughter. "Baby, I don't know what his name is. I said he's going to BE a Christian!"

Aubrey looked at me quizzically and asked, "What's a Christian?"

Seriously? Four years of dragging this kid to church, vacation Bible school, and church preschool programs and I have to tell her what a Christian is? Incredible.

"Someone who loves Jesus. Do you love Jesus?"

"Yes," she said with a skeptical look on her face.

"Then you are a Christian, too!"

She looked at me like I had lost my mind, spun on her heel, and stalked out of the room.

Aubrey was apparently under the impression that I didn't approve of Christian and was trying desperately to keep them apart because, no matter what I said to try to convince her "he" wasn't a real person, she continued to talk about him on a regular basis.

In fact, she turned down another marriage proposal from her best friend, Tristan, to continue to wait for Christian. We were playing in our neighborhood pool when Aubrey swam over to me and whispered to me, while grinning from ear to ear, "Tristan said to me, 'You're gorgeous. You're pretty. Wanna marry me?'"

I tried to remain serious, as I have learned from laughing at these types of moments that she feels I am "habing fun at her."

"What did you say?" I asked her.

"I told him, 'No way, Jose. I'm marryin' Christian,'" she said, twisting her mouth sideways to reveal one of her dimpled cheeks.

Lauren, one of our other neighborhood friends, is eleven years old, and she knows a good catch when she sees one. She tried to intervene and started playing matchmaker.

"But Aubrey," Lauren protested, "Christian isn't even a real person, and Tristan is so cute and he's your best friend!"

Aubrey's instincts were telling her to play hard to get, and the more she ignored Tristan, the louder and more extravagant his declarations of love became. I was worried things might be getting out of hand—I mean, my four-year-old shouldn't be in any hurry to make a lifelong commitment—when thankfully (for our sake, anyway) someone pooped in the swimming pool and it was time to load up and head home.

Aubrey's obsession with romance didn't end with just the idea of happily ever after, though; she became more and more enthralled with the "kissing business" she sees on her G-rated movies as well.

After watching Cinderella and Prince Charming seal their love with a kiss, she asked me, "Mommy, do we need to learn how to kiss like that?"

Lord in heaven.

"No, honey. You don't kiss boys like that until you are really, really big."

"Yeah, but you kiss Daddy like that, huh?"

"Yes, honey, I kiss Daddy like that. But I'm a grown-up, and we're married. So it's okay."

"Big kissing isn't for kids, huh, Mommy?"

"Nope," I said as I tried to nonchalantly run out of the room.

I know there will be a point when I have to discuss sexual matters with her, and honestly I'm trying to take these questions as they come. But sometimes the pressure is more than I can stand, and I have to get away to take a deep breath and come up with my best answer. I know what I would say to her if she were fourteen years old, but how much information is enough and how much is too much for a four-year-old? We all know how the whole "vagina" situation turned out . . . she knows she has one; can't that be enough for now?

When Sadie was born, my mother brought Aubrey and Emma to the hospital to see her. Emma couldn't have cared less if I'd had a baby or a litter of kittens. All she wanted was her momma. She wanted to crawl all over me in the bed (thank God my epidural was still working), and she made it quite clear she would not be leaving the hospital of her own free will without me.

Aubrey, on the other hand, was enthralled with her new baby sister. She wanted to unwrap her from her nest of blankets and count Sadie's fingers and toes. It made me smile as I remembered how my granddaddy used to hold Aubrey and do the very same thing. Aubrey wanted to know what every piece of equipment in the room was for and what every bracelet on my wrist meant. My epidural was just starting to wear off when Aubrey decided to really turn up the heat on her questions.

"Momma, how'd she get out of your belly?"

"I just pushed really hard and she popped out."

"But how, Momma?"

"Aubrey, you want some of my Popsicle?"

"How did her get out, Momma? How? Out of your belly button?"

Now, I have determined one thing for sure: I will not lie to my children. Call me crazy, but I want them to be able to trust me about things that matter, and I refuse to lie to them about insignificant things. Santa Claus and the Easter Bunny come to our house, but our kids know it's pretend and it's really Mommy and Daddy, and you can just trust me on this, they have just as much fun as anybody else on holidays. Aubrey might not be able to tell you what a Christian is, but dadgummit she knows why we celebrate Christmas and Easter.

Not that a baby coming out of your coo-coo is insignificant, mind you, but I just wasn't sure she could be trusted to keep this kind of stuff to herself. I didn't want her going to school and blurting out this new information—I might not lie to my kids, but I respect your right to do it all day long if you want to.

"MOMMA! HOW DID HER GET OUT?"

I was waiting for her to swing a delivery-room light into my face, pull up a folding chair, blow cigarette smoke at me, and ask, "Where were you on the night in question?" And I'll admit it; she had me on the ropes. I was sweating and about to cave. I was ready to give up my source, to blurt out, "MY COO-COO!" when, thankfully, a nurse came in to administer some medicine through my IV and Aubrey's preschool attention span kicked into high gear.

"Ooooh, cool! What's that?"

I was off the hook for a little while at least. Almost six months later, Aubrey was snuggling on the couch and watching TV with her daddy one evening when I overheard her ask, "Daddy, are you the one that makes my mommy all sweaty?"

I had heart palpitations and leaned against the kitchen counter to steady myself as I called to my husband, "WHAT did she just say? And why did she say it?"

My husband laughed at my obvious distress and explained that Aubrey's back was sweating where she was leaning against him. I took a few deep, cleansing breaths and prayed for a little bit more time before I had to explain "getting sweaty" to her.

30

. . . .

The Birds and the Bees

Oh God. Oh God, oh God, oh God—I thought I had more time. I thought I had years to read, do research, and ask for advice before one of my kids needed to know. I thought I would be all Clair Huxtable and take my daughters out for a special mother-daughter day to celebrate our womanhood and dish the dirt on the facts of life. I thought at the very least that my children would be capable of brushing their own teeth before we needed to talk about sex. But I was wrong, and I hate being wrong.

After Sadie's birth and Aubrey's Great Inquisition while I was still in the delivery room, I was faced with a new dilemma. Aubrey was dying to know how the baby had gotten out of my body. I did all I could to keep from lying to her and to seem like I wasn't actually avoiding the topic.

Luckily for me, for almost six months she could be easily distracted with a, "Hey, look at that! Emma has your favorite naked Barbie!" I would point to an empty corner and run into the kitchen to gulp down some Mommy Juice and hope to God she wouldn't follow me with more questions.

But she eventually wore me down. For a month Aubrey asked me at least twice a week, "Mommy, how do babies get in your tummy?" I started to feel guilty about putting her off and realized I was going to have to tell her something.

"It's a really long story," I told her the last time she asked. I was hoping to put her off at least one more time so I wouldn't have to discuss s-e-x in the car, in front of her little sister.

An hour later, Aubrey stated matter-of-factly, "I'm ready to hear that story about how babies get in your tummy now."

I realized I could no longer avoid the topic. It didn't matter that she was only five. She was in school, making friends with kids who had older siblings, and I could either answer her questions or wait until she asked someone else.

"We'll talk about it later, honey. I promise." Dammit. Being a mother is hard.

I waited until we were home and I had time to do some on-line research. I googled "what to tell your five-year-old about sex" and read all I could. I waited until Emma was distracted doing who knows what and called Aubrey into the living room by herself.

"What is it, Momma?" she asked with her eyebrows raised.

"You know how you've been asking me about how babies get into mommies' tummies?" I asked as she crawled into my lap.

Her face lit up and she nodded, excited. (Why didn't I think to pour myself a strong drink before we got into this? God help me, help me, help me, help me!)

"Well, I'm ready to talk to you about it now. It's sort of like 'potty talk.' It's not nice to talk about it with people you don't know or other children at school. Okay?"

"Like talking about my privacy . . . right, Momma?"

"That's right, baby."

I took a deep breath and dove in. "Sooo, mommies have an egg in their bellies and daddies have a seed . . ." I swallowed a little throw-up in the back of my mouth. "And the daddy puts the seed in the mommy's belly, and it makes a baby."

She smiled from ear to ear. "That is so cool, Momma!"

Oh, Lord . . . thank you! Thank you, I made it.

"But Momma . . ."

What the hell did she mean, "But Momma"? According to my Internet research, this was as far as my conversation with my five-year-old was supposed to go!

"What, baby?"

"How do the daddies get the seed in there?"

I wasn't prepared for this, but I knew that my best bet was to be as honest as possible. I took a deep, cleansing breath, tried to maintain eye contact, and said, "Well, they, um, they use their penises . . ."

I don't think I could have said anything that could have surprised her more.

Aubrey began to snicker. "Their PENISES?" Once she started laughing, there was no stopping her. She laughed until she was doubled over in my lap, wheezing with tears squeezing out the corners of her eyes.

"Are you for real, Momma?"

By this point, I was pretty tickled, too, and all I could do was nod.

"OH MY GOSH! THAT IS SO SILLY! They just poke it in your belly?"

I nodded again . . . I mean, really—enough is enough.

Once we were able to get ourselves together, I asked her seriously, "Aubrey, did that answer all of your questions?"

"Yep."

"Good. I want you to know that if you ever have any questions about anything, you can come to me. Understand? No matter what it is, I'll always be ready to talk to you and help you."

"Okay, Mommy."

I said another silent "Dear God, please!" prayer, held my breath, and asked, "Do you have anything else you want to ask me?"

Aubrey matched my tone perfectly as she stared into my eyes and said seriously, "No. Did you have anything else you wanted to tell me?"

No, actually, after telling my five-year-old how babies are made—I think I've pretty much said everything I want to say for this evening . . . except for maybe, "Pass the Mommy Juice."

Mall Madness

I would like to formally apologize to anyone who found themselves in Northwoods Mall in Charleston, South Carolina, on August 24, 2009, at approximately 12:47 P.M. That eardrum-rupturing scream you heard for a full fifteen minutes? That was my kid.

My mother was in town visiting and needed to go shopping for clothes to wear to my younger brother's wedding. It was Aubrey's first day of kindergarten, so I thought it would be a special treat to take Emma to the mall for lunch and a little playtime on the mall's indoor play area.

Emma is my wild child, but on this morning she was being a complete angel. She walked beside our Sit N Stand stroller as I pushed Sadie through the stores and only hid in a rack of clothes twice. Every time I asked her to stop touching something, she immediately replied, "Okay. I wee-ill, Momma." She held my hand, said "please" and "thank you," and smiled at the Dead Sea

Minerals chicks as they verbally assaulted us every time we passed them. "Miss, excuse me . . . Miss, can I ask you a question?"

We ate lunch in the food court, and I'll admit I was getting a little smug about how wonderful my children were behaving. I don't know what it is about having kids, but no matter how many you have, having one less seems like the easiest thing in the world. You have one baby, and you can barely make it through the day. But once you have a second child, you realize how easy it actually was. And anytime you have one fewer, you feel like you're on vacation.

That's exactly how I was feeling as we ate lunch. I actually said out loud (but, thankfully, only to my mother, who has raised three babies and probably knew I was going to eat my words), "Oh my goodness, this is so nice! Emma, Sadie, and I might start coming up here more often; she's playing so well and minding. I'm so glad school has started back!"

Cue the kamikaze death spiral.

Emma was not impressed when it was time to leave the play area and was determined to twist the knob of every gumball machine until something came out, even though she hadn't put any money in the machine. I coaxed, cajoled, begged, and—I'm not ashamed to admit it—bribed.

She finally agreed to release her death grip on the gumball machine when I produced a lollipop out of my diaper bag. About the time the lollipop disappeared, we were in the Dillard's shoe department watching my mother try on shoes. Or trying to watch, anyway.

Quick soapbox here: if you don't want mothers to shop in your store, just put a sign on the front door that says "Keep Your Brats to Yourself" or some such thing, because nothing—

nothing—irritates me more than to be in a store trying to shop and the aisles are not wide enough for a stroller to fit through. I would prefer that you just save me some time and a whole arsenal of cuss words and give it to me straight.

Back to my story . . . I was cussing under my breath so Momma and Emma wouldn't hear me, while attempting to maneuver my stroller close enough to see Momma's shoes and give an opinion. It was getting close to nap time, and I was getting worried. Emma needs naps like Lindsay Lohan needs the paparazzi—she cannot survive without them.

Lucky for Emma, the shoe department was conveniently located right next to the linens. And there was a colorful display bed, there for the taking. Emma climbed onto the display rack and belly flopped onto the bed. I was pinned between two racks of shoes and my stroller and couldn't reach her. My mother had on two different shoes, a wedge sandal and a ballet flat, and was limping across the shoe department to try to get to Emma. But before either of us could grab her, Emma climbed under the covers and jerked them over her head, sending the plastic sale signs clattering to the floor.

I finally extricated myself from my roadblock and pulled Emma out of the bed just as a helpful sales clerk came to see if my momma needed any help and to give me the stink-eye. I recognized her "when I have children, they will behave!" look and just went right ahead and laughed in her face. "Guess it's nap time!" I joked as I made the bed and replaced the signs. She rolled her eyes at me and walked away just as Emma twisted out of my grip and jumped back into the bed.

This time I was ready. There was no stroller blocking my path, and I lunged for her, which was the first in a series of

Road Runner and Wile E. Coyote–ish moves that lead to Emma and me darting and weaving around kiosks of purses, belts, and accessories. The child is fast.

I darted one way, and she would dash the other, keeping a wall of merchandise between us at all times.

"Emma Jean O'Bryant! You'd better come here RIGHT NOW! Do you hear me?" (Her name is actually Emma Rachel after my momma, but when she's bad I call her Emma Jean and always have. It's her evil redneck alter ego.)

"MOMMA, DON'T 'PANK ME!! PWEASE, MOMMA, DON'T!"

Well, chit. If I was going to, I'm not now, because now everyone in the store is staring at us, and I personally don't have the time to talk to Child Protective Services and explain my disciplining techniques.

Momma finally got her own shoes back on and helped me block Emma in near a rack of costume jewelry. As soon as I was within reach of her, I picked her up.

"Emma. Get in the stroller. We are going home," I said, maintaining eye contact and low tones.

"I WANNA WALK!!! STOP TOUCHING ME! YOU AH HUTTING ME!" she screamed at full volume.

"Emma, if you do not sit down in the stroller, right now, I will strap you in. Do you understand?"

I was walking now and holding her as she continued to writhe, scream, and generally make a public spectacle of herself. My mother pushed the stroller along behind me, several feet behind me if I remember correctly. Like she didn't even know us and certainly wasn't with us. As soon as we were out of the store, I knelt in front of Emma and once again gave her the choice to sit willingly in the stroller or be strapped in.

"I WANT TO WAAAAAAAAALLLK!" she shrieked.

I'm not even sure if I can accurately explain how loud she was. I am not exaggerating when I say that every single person in the mall heard her, and many people walked out of stores to see what was going on. My children have pitched fits before in public, but never, ever like this.

Emma wouldn't cooperate, so I put her in the stroller and strapped her in while she straightened her arms and legs and bowed her back to try to keep from being put into the seat.

She was actually in the seat belt for less than fifteen seconds before she pulled a Houdini, jumped out of the moving stroller, and took off running in the opposite direction.

I gave chase, and when I caught her, I held her around her tiny waist while she kicked me and screamed at me. She was thrashing. Had I not been so completely and totally shocked at her behavior, I would have been mortified, but at this point I could think of only one thing: getting the hell out of there.

Of course, we were as far from my car as we could possibly be and still be in the mall. I was forced to walk/run the entire length of the mall carrying my feral child. At one point, my shirt had ridden up to my bra line, Emma was upside down with her feet over my head, her dress over her head and her panties half off of her booty as I struggled to keep her in my arms.

I kept waiting for security or a concerned citizen to stop me and ask, "Is this your child?" My plan was to say, "Never seen her before," pass her off to the well-meaning stranger, and high-tail it out of there, but no one approached us. No one had anything to say to me. Not even the Dead Sea Minerals chick, which really, really pissed me off.

"WHAT?" I yelled at her kiosk. "What was your question?

Doesn't seem so important now, does it?? What!? You don't want me to stop and talk now, do you?"

She wisely avoided eye contact and said nothing.

Finally, finally, we made it to my car. My mother's feet were covered in blisters from running the length of the mall while pushing a double stroller, and Emma had completely worn herself out pitching the World's Biggest Hissy Fit. My mother slipped off her shoes in the passenger seat as Emma whimpered herself to sleep and I wished to God I had thought to pack a sippy cup of Mommy Juice in the diaper bag.

Why It's All Worth It

I had a really great childhood. My teenage years were full of angst, turmoil, and my parents' divorce, but as far as childhoods go, I had a great one. I grew up in a small, close-knit town, and I have wonderful memories of backyard barbecues, fish fries, and birthday parties with friends. (In the South, a barbecue is when you cook actual barbecue, not just when you throw anything on a grill. That would be a "cookout," as in, "We're cooking outside.")

The sounds and smells of Alabama in the summertime still bring back a flood of memories: a lick of wild honeysuckle, running barefoot through freshly cut grass, charcoal burning on a grill, crickets singing and frogs croaking while we chased each other through muscadine vines and fig trees playing hide-and-seek (or "seek and destroy," as the boys called it, because once they found you, they basically beat the crap out of you), all the moms bustling around in the kitchen getting side dishes ready while the men sipped cold beers around the grill.

My mom's best friend, Linda Murphy, lived right through

the woods. My brothers, my sister, and I spent countless hours walking a path through the woods to see the Murphy family next door. We did everything with them: we went to the beach, to Smith Lake, to Disney World. The first time I remember spending the night away from home was at their house.

So many of my happiest memories are intertwined with memories of them; they were as close as siblings. We fought, laughed, and cried together. We swung each other in our hammock to see if we could flip it 360 degrees, then bandaged each other's wounds when we realized that in hand-to-hand combat with the law of gravity, we would lose every time. We made stupid home videos dressed up with wigs and heinous 80s accessories. My older brother, Matt, acted as our lead singer while we made up dance routines so horrible I can only thank God there was no YouTube back then.

Their second child, Lawson, is the first baby I ever remember holding. Some of my memories of Lawson are so vivid, I can flip through them in my mind as if they were snapshots instead . . . perfectly detailed without the fogginess that sometimes surrounds my childhood memories. When Lawson was only a few months old, my brother Matt was lying on the floor playing "airplane" with him. Lawson was giggling that effervescent baby giggle that had everyone in the room, including my teenage brother, laughing. Matt held him upside down for a little too long and was still laughing, mouth wide open, when Lawson threw up in it.

I remember being completely and totally grossed out by the skid marks in his first pair of "big boy" underwear. And I remember watching Lawson and his younger brother John play "rough and tumble" in their tiny Auburn football jerseys in the Murphys' living room until one of them inevitably ended up flying headfirst into the coffee table.

I only have two real memories of my first trip to Disney World. One of them was being involved in some sort of silly street play, but the other is of Lawson at our hotel swimming pool. He was trying to "flatfoot it" and see if he could touch the bottom of the deep end of the pool.

When I turned sixteen, I drove him and "the girl next door" to Maddox Middle School basketball games in my supercool maroon Oldsmobile, the Hot Tamale. I teased him unmercifully all the way to her house. "I can't believe you have a girlfriend."

"She is NOT my girlfriend!"

"She is SO your girlfriend!"

"She is NOT! And you better stop when she gets in the car."

I kept my mouth shut once she got in the car, and we cranked up the music and rocked out to Weezer the rest of the way there.

Lawson and I traded CDs and, years later, called each other on occasion to blast our favorite parts at each other, hanging up without saying a word.

When I got married and moved out of state, Lawson and I didn't talk for several years. But then my phone rang, and it was as if no time had passed at all. Lawson had just started Auburn—the college of his dreams. I was living in Auburn, too—busy being married, working, and finishing nursing school.

"Hello?"

Music blasted in my ear. "IF I HAD MY TIME AGAIN, I WOULD DO IT ALL THE SAAA-AA-AME!" Big Audio Dynamite sang through the phone.

"HEY! That's mine!! I've been looking for it for five years!" I yelled into the phone.

"Yeah? Well when you cough up my Weezer CD, you can have it back." Lawson bartered.

"LAW! You know that CD got destroyed in the Hot Tamale!

Seriously, I'll buy you a new one . . . or I'll cook for you if you give it back!"

We both made good on our bargain, and the CD bought him a couple of meals a month as I continued to play the big-sister role and cook for him to give him a break from college life.

He came over one evening for chili and Mexican cornbread that was a poor imitation of our mommas' version.

"Sorry." I kept apologizing to him and Zeb as I checked the cornbread repeatedly. I had doubled the recipe and used a glass dish and seriously underestimated the baking time.

Every time I walked past Lawson into the kitchen to check the oven, he coughed, "Ah-huh-ROOKIE-huh!"

The night Lawson came over for chili and cornbread would be the last time I would ever see him. He was only eighteen.

I was twenty-five years old and on vacation with my dad, step-mother, brothers, and my sister. There weren't any grandchildren yet. We were at the beach six hours from home when Mary Beth, Lawson's older sister, called my sister Blair's cell phone.

I wasn't even awake on the morning when she stumbled into my room crying. "There was an accident at the lake, and they can't find Lawson," Blair choked out.

They couldn't find him. They couldn't find him. If he couldn't be found, then he couldn't be gone, I reasoned. They would find him. Wouldn't they?

The day was a blur. I remember it as though in a postanes-thesia fog. I felt drugged. My dad drove my sister and me home. I remember buying a Diet Coke and powdered donuts at a gas station because they were by the counter and I had to eat some-thing. It seemed ridiculous to eat donuts when someone I loved was probably dead, but I had no idea what else to eat, so I grabbed them. I don't remember calling my mother, though I suppose I did. I don't remember where Zeb was. I know he was at the beach with me, but I don't remember him being in the car that day as we drove north.

We made our way to the lake, to our other family, and were told: Lawson had been found.

He was found, but lost forever. Gone, but home.

I cried so hard I thought my heart would actually shatter as we drove back across Duncan Bridge. The lake sparkled in the sunlight; the baby-blue beams of the bridge almost disappeared into the sky over my head. I remembered the hundreds of times as a child that we had ridden in a boat underneath that bridge, screaming at the top of our lungs just to hear the echo. But our voices were one less now. Lawson's was gone, but I still wanted to scream.

My grief was physical. It hurt and throbbed and ached. I could not fathom the actual pain a mother feels to lose a child or that a sibling feels to lose a soul mate. How could the rest of us be expected to go on and just live, without him?

Lawson was the first person I had ever loved, wholeheartedly, from the moment he entered this world—until the moment he left it.

What I wanted to do when I "grew up" changed on a regular basis. There was an astronaut phase, a doctor phase, and a lawyer phase. But what I wanted to be remained constant. I wanted to be a wife and a mother and to have a family of my own: a family to take to the lake and Disney World and to spend lazy days in a hammock with.

When Lawson died, I didn't know if I could do that anymore. I questioned myself and God as I tried to make sense of his death. I thought I would never be able to survive the pain a mother endures when she loses a child. The risk of losing something so precious might not be worth the heartache it could potentially bring.

Until one day I found myself thinking what my life would have been like without Lawson. My life would have been worth living, but I wouldn't have laughed as hard or as often. I realized how much I would have missed out on if he had not been a part of my life. All of the laughter and good times were a tribute to him. Life is about making as much joy as you possibly can out of the situations you find yourself in.

I used to be a type-A Control Freak. I worried constantly, especially when things didn't go according to my plan. But you cannot enjoy life that way. Life is loving and losing people. Losing Lawson taught me that nothing is forever and that every moment counts.

All the screaming, dirty diapers, tantrum throwing, and sleepless nights are worth it. It is worth every heartache and tear we shed as mothers. It is worth every labor pain, every hemorrhoid, and every humiliating weigh-in at the doctor's office as your weight skyrockets to numbers usually reserved for linebackers and heavyweight champs.

Because every moment counts.

I find myself thinking of Lawson from time to time, sometimes when I least expect it. I'll give Emma a big push on the tire swing and remember spinning upside down on a hammock with him, all of our siblings drunk with laughter. I'll watch Aubrey and her best buddy, John Heston, sword fighting with sticks until one of them is bleeding and crying, and I am transported through time to the Murphys' red brick patio, wiping blood off of Lawson's knee and plastering a Teenage Mutant Ninja Turtle Band-Aid on his war wound.

Sadie cries out in the middle of the night, and as I stumble through the darkness to her room, often before I can even think, "I wish I was still asleep," I'll have the thought, "Lawson never got to do this."

He is on my mind as I walk into Sadie's darkened room, and I smile as I see her. Her smile is so big and so automatic that her eyes crinkle and her pacifier falls out of her mouth, revealing her gummy little mouth. I pick her up, glad to have the time to snuggle with her while the rest of the world sleeps. The inconvenience of being pulled from my warm bed is forgotten.

I climb into my rocking chair to feed her. She nestles against me with one hand propped up on my chest and her other arm wrapped around my side. She closes her eyes so tightly she looks as though she is faking sleep . . . playing possum.

Her face is my past and my future. I see my own baby pictures as I look at her button nose and MoonPie face, as round as if God drew it with a compass. I see my grandmother in the arch of her eyebrows, "the McNeal eyebrow," she called it. I see my older daughters and know that God didn't break the mold when He made them. He found one so perfect, He decided to use it three times.

"Lawson never got to do this," I think as a rogue tear slips down my cheek. He didn't get to see his own reflection in another person. He didn't get to look for his family in his child's face.

As I look at Sadie's sleeping profile, I see Blair, my sister and best friend, her imitation so perfect I want to whisper one of our childhood secrets in Sadie's tiny ear. "Lawson would have made you laugh," I say softly instead.

Sadie has my mother's lips, and as I gaze at her tiny face, it makes me wonder whose voice will come out of her mouth when she starts to talk. She stops nursing, milk dribbling down a chin kissed with her daddy's dimple and hinting of her Pop Pete.

She sighs.

I sigh to inhale her sweet baby's breath. I prop her on my shoulder to examine her more closely and to nuzzle the warmth of her cheeks.

My child. Lawson will never get to say that.

Her hand swipes at my face; before I tuck it into her blanket, I see her hands and fingernails are scale reproductions of her daddy's. I wonder about all the things she will use them for . . . sword fights, pushing swings, picking muscadines, and plucking the stem out of a honeysuckle bloom. Will she get the chance to hold her own child?

Lawson didn't.

I groan as I rise from my chair to place her back in her crib, her head on my shoulder . . . her hand on my heart.

Every moment counts.

Every child that is brought into this world is a miracle and gift from God. The fact that two imperfect human beings can create another life is almost inconceivable—especially once you have witnessed the fragility, innocence, and perfection of a newborn, when you have held your own child's helpless body, seen her open her mouth like a tiny little bird, trusting that someone will feed her, because without you she cannot survive.

Every child that is born fills me full of hope. Hope that this world isn't the horrible place depicted on the evening news. Hope that if something so perfect can even exist, then there is good to be found in the world.

Every child is another opportunity for us to get things right, to raise our children with a respect for God and people and with a zest for life. Every day brings a new opportunity to love our children, to laugh with them, cry with them, and watch them grow. Every day with our children is an opportunity for us to learn from them, to hopefully replicate their easy acceptance of others and unconditional love for life. Every day there is an opportunity to let God use your children to sand off your own rough edges, making you more like them and ultimately more like Him.

It can be difficult to keep these things in perspective.

Life is semisweet, for sure. There is bitterness there, like medicine mixed in chocolate syrup, and it must be swallowed whole along with the moments that flood your heart with pure joy. We can laugh, or we can cry. The choice is yours. But if I had my time again—I'd do it all the same.

Acknowledgments

This is where I'm supposed to thank all the "little people" who made this book possible, but the truth is, aside from the shorties in my house, all the people who have supported me are larger than life.

To my parents: Hank and Rachel Wiley—thank you for loving me unconditionally and taking me to the library and to Waldenbooks, where your twenty bucks barely lasted twenty-four hours.

Shuggie, you are the best mother and grandmother anyone could ever have. Ever.

Daddy, you have never been more than a phone call away.

To my brothers, Matt Wiley and Bebo Dutton: I wouldn't have wanted to grow up being beaten down by anyone else. To Pete and Tom Wiley: read, read, read—then tell me all about it.

To the Farm People: thanks for letting me be one of y'all. Best in-laws ever.

To my sister, Blair Martin: you complete me. Seriously. Jerry Maguire stole that line from me. I don't have to say anything here to make you cry. I know you're going to do that every time you see my REAL LIVE book. Thank you for believing in me, always.

Huge thanks to Dana Frazeur, Peyton Kennedy, and Blair Martin, who have literally read every word I've ever written—over and over and over again. Thank you for telling me when it didn't work and for cheering me on when it did and for making me put myself "out there." Thanks to Kathryn Dyksterhouse for proofreading while on bed rest and for being the first person to welcome me to Greenwood.

One million thanks to Peyton, brilliant editor and amazing friend, who helped me polish this manuscript to a high shine. And to Miki McCurdy for taking fabulous pictures and editing them at lightning speed.

Thanks to my agent, Jenny Bent, for seeing potential in me, for helping me find my voice, and for having the patience of Job. The fact that you believe in me and think I'm funny makes me almost believe it myself.

Thank you to my closest friends: Lizzie Powers (aka Sister Wife) for helping me raise my kids, waxing my eyebrows, and saving me thousands of dollars' worth of psychotherapy. And to the LOLers: Blair Martin, Kasey Colvin, Natalie Brown, Peyton Kennedy, and Stacey Hamner—I couldn't have asked for a better support group. You sickens literally make me LOL every day and help me keep perspective when I'm having those Debbie Downer–type of days. To Amy Dill for being my 1-800-Dial-a-Friend ever since I could hold a phone.

To the writing community, especially my Tweeps: I never knew that writers were such nice people until I started pretending I was one of you. Thanks for playing along with me and for giving me advice, responding to my e-mails, and making me feel normal.

To Celia Rivenbark, Stefanie Wilder-Taylor, and Jenny Lawson: for being more gracious than I ever could have imagined in my wildest dreams, and trust me—I've dreamed about knowing y'all for a long time.

To my friends and family I've collected in my travels: Gena James, Connie and Buck Whitmire and family, my Tuesday-morning Bible-study girls, and my family at WPC. You can never know how much your love, support, and friendship have meant to me.

To my readers: thank you, thank you, thank you! Thank you for every e-mail, every comment, and every shared story. I love being a part of your life and it's because of you that all of my dreams have come true

And last but certainly not least: Zeb, Aubrey, Emma, and Sadie: I wouldn't want to do this with anybody else.

Read on for a bonus sneak peek at Robin's next book . . .

Are You There, God? It's Me, Mommy

Copyright © 2014 by Robin O'Bryant.

Introduction

This is not a devotional. If that's what you're looking for, you should stop reading right now, because I have more questions than I have answers. My life is not perfect, and neither am I. I'm trying hard to get this whole motherhood thing right, but most of the time I find myself flailing around and praying that I won't scar my children for life.

This isn't a book about how you *should* live your life; it's a book about how I'm trying to live mine. I am human. I make mistakes all of the time, but I am trying desperately to get it right—the balance of work and home, husband and kids, the world against the Word.

I struggle every day. I try to find time for everything I'm supposed to do: meet my children's needs, exercise, throw something together for dinner every night, not spend all my money at Target on crap that I don't need, not call my husband names when he brushes my babies' teeth with her sister's toothbrush,

not talk about/murder in cold blood the mom who keeps post-
ing on Facebook that her child was puking last night, then
brings the kid to school the next morning. I try to breathe, try
to pray, try to be a good person, a good mother, and a decent
Christian—I'm doing the best I can, but so many times I get it
wrong. I fail.

I lose my temper when I shouldn't. I do my Bible-study homework in the car before I walk into the church for our weekly
meeting—if I bother to go at all. I yell cuss words at other
mothers who cut me off in the carpool line, and I feed my kids
overprocessed chicken nuggets at least once (*read: twice*) a week.

Most of the devotionals I've read seem lofty and almost impossible to me. After growing up in the church and attending
Bible school for two years, I'd read and heard a shit ton about
how I *should* live my life. And all of that information about what
I should be doing became a crushing and constant reminder of
how I didn't measure up. I wasn't spiritual enough. I cussed too
much. I didn't do my quiet time. I hated vacation Bible school,
but I still loved Jesus and didn't like feeling like a disappointment to Him.

This is not a book about how you *should* live your life. I'm
not going to tell you how spiritual I am or try to paint myself as
a model of modern spirituality because that would be a fla-
grant lie.

I'm simply going to tell you my story. The story of how God
took me—a *wildly* imperfect woman—and showed me, through
the amazing love of my husband and the jolting experiences of
motherhood, that I was enough. That He loved me in my sin,
that He loved me in my flaws and the personality quirks that I'd
mistakenly labeled "sin," and that there was nothing I could do
to earn it or deserve it.

God has proved to me, time and time again, that He is still relevant and that His love never fails. At the risk of your thinking I'm a bad Christian—or, even worse, a bad mother—here is my story. . . .

Hello, My Name Is "Aubrey's Mom"?

Dear God,

I've always wanted to be a mother, but I didn't know it was going to be like this. I didn't realize I was going to feel so lost. I didn't know the rest of my life was going to come to a screeching halt. I thought I would still be "me" but with kids . . . I didn't realize that there was no "rest of my life" after having kids. Changing diapers, making bottles, saying "No," screaming "No," singing "No," crying "No"—is this what my life is supposed to look like now?

I'm not just "Robin" anymore. I'm "Aubrey's mom," and I don't even know who she is.

Me

I walked into the church fellowship hall and did a quick scan of the room while I waited for a name tag. I tried to get a feel for the moms present so that I wouldn't look like an idiot standing by the door blocking the flow of women. I was looking for a particular kind of someone, but I didn't yet have a name or face yet, just the idea of a Mommy Soul Mate.

I needed a mom in a semicute outfit, spit-up stains optional, with a stylish diaper bag, funky sunglasses, and a snarky sense of humor. I needed a mom who wasn't going to judge me for not liking breastfeeding, a mom who let her kids eat Popsicles and occasionally dirt, and a mom who would reassure me that I was capable of caring for two children under two years old. *That* was going to be my new best friend, but I wasn't sure how I was going to spot her.

After three months of being stuck in the house in a new city, with no friends, no job, no coworkers, and no way to meet people, I was becoming desperate. I needed adult conversation like my toddler needed her favorite stuffed animal, and, just like Aubrey, I wasn't above throwing a fit to get what I wanted.

This MOPs (Mothers of Preschoolers) meeting was my first big chance to make a friend. Someone to talk to throughout the day while my husband was at work. Someone to meet at the mall so I didn't feel like such a loser eating Chick-fil-A in the food court with just a two-year-old and a baby bump to keep me company. (Honestly, calling it a bump is much too kind. I looked like Homer Simpson, donut in hand, hairy belly button and all. Doh!)

I didn't want to waste time with a bunch of moms who didn't "get me." I wanted to find my Mommy Soul Mate, and I wasn't above a little social profiling to get it. I got my name tag and slid into a seat at a table full of supercute mommies. This was it. This was my chance to make a friend. *Maybe I would even make more than one!* Oh, the excitement! I could just see myself, texting all of my friends, meeting them for dinner for a Girls' Nights Out. This was going to be fabulous.

"Hey, Robin! How are you? Are you new to Savannah?" a cute blonde asked, reading my name tag.

"I am. We just moved here a few months ago."

"I see you're expecting! Congrats! Any other kids?"

"I have a two-year-old, Aubrey, and another girl on the way." I returned her questions about her kids. Things were going pretty well. I was feeling good about our potential relationship. She hadn't named her kids Moonbeam or Solar Plexus. We could totally be friends.

"So what do you do?" she asked.

"Um, I used to be an ER nurse, but now I'm just staying home with Aubrey?" I answered. I had only been staying home since our move, and when I told people what I "did" it came out as a question. As if I needed some stranger's permission to be a stay-at-home mother.

"Oh, that's cool. What do you like to do?"

"I . . . uh . . . um . . . I . . . don't . . ."

What the hell was wrong with me? My heart started racing, and sweat beads formed on my upper lip. Think, Robin! Make words! Think!

I couldn't say, "Well, most days I try to stay in my pajamas until my husband comes home from work. Occasionally, I'll put on a bra, but for the most part I like to let the girls dangle free. I like to see how many days I can go without washing my hair, because I'm too tired to lift my arms over my head after I get my kid in bed. AND I only sweep my floors about once a week, 'cause what's the point with a toddler in the house? Right? Am I right?" (Insert cheesy wink.) "I can eat up to ten Double Stuf Oreos in one sitting, and I've seen every episode ever made of *Law & Order: SVU*. I'm an insomniac, and what's not to love about a show focused solely on sexual deviants and murder, right? RIGHT?"

I was totally stumped. Not only did I not know what I liked to do, but I had no idea when I had last given a single thought to what my interests might be.

Apparently, my five-minute pause in conversation and glazed-over eyes translated as "I'm a little off in the head," and my potential Mommy Soul Mate started drifting.

"I like to read!" I yelled as she simultaneously said, "Nice to meet you," and got up from the table to go talk to one of her friends across the room.

The sweet-looking brunette next to me smiled. "Do I recognize you from the Soft Play at the mall?"

"Probably." I smiled back. "I'm Aubrey's mom."

That's when it hit me like a ton of bricks. Not only did I not have any idea what I was interested in, I no longer had a name. I was now officially "Aubrey's mom." I was barely two years in to this whole motherhood thing, and I didn't even think of myself in terms of *me* anymore. I thought of myself as their momma.

Instead of glowing with joy at the life I was carrying and being proud to be the mother of a beautiful and healthy daughter, I felt empty. I was the shell of what a mother is supposed to be. I was a Stepford wife, except instead of having perfectly coiffed hair, a matching cardigan set, and a roast in the oven with a kitchen timer that would ding just as my husband walked in the door from work, I'd had on the same maternity outfit I'd been wearing for the last two years. I'd barely had time to lose my baby weight after having Aubrey before I was pregnant again. I had dark circles under my eyes, and my roots were a half inch long in a sloppy ponytail that wouldn't stay pulled out of my face—probably because I had used a toddler-sized rubber hair band. Dinner was just as likely to be takeout as it was leftovers—you have lots of leftovers when you only have one kid that's barely eating solid foods and you are compulsively googling recipes for family dinners because you have nothing else to do all day.

The idea of being a "stay-at-home mom" had been so appealing before I was actually doing it. When I was working as an ER nurse, I longed to be home with Aubrey. My heart ached to take her to the park and teach her the alphabet and the colors of the friggin' rainbow. Then I started to stay at home and realized that all of the above took up approximately an hour of our life. The other twenty-three hours would be spent digging crayons out of her mouth, watching Elmo, and making sure she didn't poke herself in the eye with a sharp stick.

Introducing myself as "Aubrey's mom" made me feel somehow defective. I wasn't even convinced yet that Aubrey wouldn't be better off in day care where people weren't tempted to watch *Law & Order* reruns all day while halfheartedly playing blocks with her. I mean, sure, she knew enough about police procedure to secure a crime scene and make a good witness if a case went to trial, but why didn't that feel like enough?

I was boring. I bored myself, and in that moment, I couldn't imagine anyone on the planet wanting to have a conversation with me.

That day in the church fellowship hall was just the beginning of my realization that being a mother would forever change how I saw myself. For the last seven years I have become someone else entirely.

I am "Aubrey's mom," "Emma's mom," "Sadie's mom," and "Zeb's wife." I am the cook. I am the grocery shopper. I am the chauffeur. I am the washer of clothes and the cleaner-upper of all bodily fluids. I am the tooth brusher, the Tooth Fairy, Santa Claus, and the Queen of Time-Outs. I am the kisser of boo-boos and the referee of fights. I am on call twenty-four hours a day, seven days a week, but I find that I am hardly ever just Robin anymore.

It would be impossible to forget, even for a second, that my family is my new identity. Any moment taken to have a free-formed thought of my own is interrupted by "Momma! Momma! Momma! MOM-MA! MOMMMMEEEEE!" I am the mother of three, and the constant chorus of three little sopranos is the sound track of my life.

They chant my new name until I snap, "WHAAT?"

"Ummm . . ." Now that Emma has my attention, she looks for something worthwhile to say. "I wub you."

I sigh. "I love you, too."

I love my kids. I wouldn't go back to being "just Robin" if I could, but I vaguely remember the bliss of a simple existence—being me with no strings attached. No 3:00 A.M. wake-up calls, no 5:00 A.M. demands for pancakes, no one hogging my remote when I want to watch TV, and the luxury of feeding only myself at meal time.

I've been completely and totally consumed by my children and the beast that is motherhood.

I suppose the woman I once was is still lurking inside me somewhere, but I'm so busy and so tired, I'm not even really sure what she wants anymore.

In the day-to-day drama of motherhood, I *need* desperately to know who I am. What happened to the girl who dreamed of being an astronaut, an actress, and a writer? That girl who used to make everyone laugh and who spent hours in front of the mirror pretending to be interviewed by Arsenio Hall? The girl who just assumed that, somehow, someday, she would be rele-vant. She would really matter; people would want to know what she thought and how she felt. Where'd *she* go?

I couldn't find her at the grocery store or at the bottom of the laundry hamper. She wasn't doing a perp walk on *Law & Order: SVU,* and she wasn't sitting with me in the carpool line. I couldn't remember the last time I'd seen or heard from that girl, and I was panicked. Was my worth really measured by the things I did for my family? Had motherhood literally eaten the rest of my dreams alive?

C. S. Lewis said, "Christ died for men precisely because men are not worth dying for; to make them worth it." When I am having a total identity crisis, questioning my worth and my purpose, I have to remember that I am His. I am worth something because He who is worth everything made the choice to die for me. Through the gift of Jesus, God showed me that I have worth and value. His love for me gives me worth, identity, and purpose, and not because of what I do or whose mother I am. No. God's love is for me in my simplest form. God's love is for "just Robin" and is not based on what I can or will do for Him.

I knew this, but I didn't understand it. The moment in the church fellowship hall was only a hint of the struggles I was going to face as I tried to figure out who the hell I was if I wasn't ever going to be "just Robin" again.